THE BOOK OF
CATHOLIC WISDOM

Also by Msgr. Dollen

Prayer Book of the Saints
Prayers for the Third Age

THE BOOK OF
CATHOLIC WISDOM

MSGR. CHARLES DOLLEN
Editor

Our Sunday Visitor Publishing Division
Our Sunday Visitor, Inc.
Huntington, Indiana 46750

Library of Congress Catalog Number: 86-60327
International Standard Book Number: 0-87973-535-X

Cover design by James E. McIlrath

Printed in the United States of America

535

For Father Bernard F. Dollen
Pastor
St. John of Rochester Church
Perinton
Fairport, N.Y.

Acknowledgments

Some material was newly translated for this volume. I have also drawn heavily on my notes and materials for my previous anthologies:

A Voice Said Ave! St. Paul Editions.
Jesus Lord. St. Paul Editions.
Civil Rights. A Source-Book. St. Paul Editions.
The Catholic Tradition (14 vols.). Consortium.
Prayer Book of the Saints. Our Sunday Visitor.
Prayers for the Third Age. Our Sunday Visitor.
Marmion: Fire of Love. B. Herder.
Ready or Not. St. Paul Editions.

Besides individual titles of writers included herein, the following have been useful:

Butler. *Lives of the Saints.* Kenedy.
Breviarium Romanum. Herder.
Britt. *Hymns of the Breviary and Missal.* Burns, Oates & Washbourne.
The Catholic Encyclopedia. (Old and New Editions.)
Carlen. *The Papal Encyclicals.* Consortium.
Chapin. *The Book of Catholic Quotations.* Farrar, Straus & Cudahy.
Cook. *101 Famous Poems.* Reilly & Lee.
Cox. *The Handbook of Christian Spirituality.* Harper & Row.
Fathers of the Church. Catholic University Press.
Fathers of the Church. Newman Press.
I.C.E.L. *Liturgy of the Hours.* Catholic Book Publishing Co.
Kilmer. *Anthology of Catholic Poets.* Liveright.
Magill. *Masterpieces of Catholic Literature.* Harper & Row.
Mead. *The Encyclopedia of Religious Quotations.* Revell.
Pennington. *The Last of the Fathers.* St. Bede's.
Ramsey. *Beginning to Read the Fathers.* Paulist Press.

The Sixteen Documents of Vatican II. St. Paul Editions.
Willis. *The Teachings of the Church Fathers.* Palm.

I also acknowledge a debt to the following publishers for brief
excerpts from works and authors cited below:

America Press, *Interracial Justice* by John LaFarge, S.J.; Christian
Classics, *Agapē in the New Testament* by Ceslaus Spicq;
Daughters of St. Paul, *Mary, Hope of the World* by James
Alberione; Desclée et Brouwer, *The Church of the Word Incarnate*
by Charles Journet; Doubleday, *Models of the Church* by Avery
Dulles, *Confessions of a Guilty Bystander* by Thomas Merton,
Morality for Our Time by Marc Oraison, and *The Church and the
Catholic* by Romano Guardini ; Duquesne University Press, *Faith
and the World* by Albert Dondeyne; Farrar, Straus & Giroux,
Disputed Questions by Thomas Merton; Franciscan Herald Press,
Transformation in Christ by Dietrich Von Hildebrand; Harper &
Row, *The Divine Milieu* by Pierre Teilhard de Chardin; Henry
Regnery, *The Lord* by Romano Guardini; Liturgical Press, *Dry
Bones* by Robert Hovda; Macmillan, *The Spirit of Catholicism* by
Karl Adam, *The New Church* by Daniel Callahan, *The Power and
the Wisdom* and *The Two-Edged Sword* by John L. McKenzie;
Paulist Press, *Hermeneutics* by Raymond Brown, *Lay People in the
Church* by Yves Congar, and *The Law of Christ* by Bernard
Häring; Pickwick Press, *Love and the Person* by Maurice
Nedoncelle; Scribner, *Moral Philosophy* by Jacques Maritain;
Seabury Crossroad Books, *Jesus and the Gospels* by Pierre Benoit,
Christian Theology of St. Paul by Lucien Cerfaux, various titles by
Karl Rahner, *Christian Existence in the New Testament* by Rudolf
Schackenburg, and *Corresponsibility in the Church* by Léon-
Joseph Cardinal Suenens; Sheed, Andrews & McMeel, *The
Resurrection* by Francis X. Durrwell, *Christ in the Christian
Tradition* by Aloys Grillmeier, and *Christ, the Sacrament of
Encounter with God* by Edward Schillebeeckx; Sheed & Ward, *The
Spirit of the Liturgy* by Romano Guardini, plus titles by Hilaire
Belloc, G.K. Chesterton, Caryll Houselander, Arnold Lunn, Frank
Sheed, and Maisie Ward; University of Chicago Press, *American*

Catholicism by John Tracy Ellis and *Man and the State* by Jacques Maritain; the University of Notre Dame Press for *Liturgical Piety* by Louis Bouyer and *Poustinia* by Catherine de Hueck Doherty; and the Universal Features Syndicate for an excerpt from a column by Andrew M. Greeley. We have been unable to verify some of the publishers. Anyone with information on publishers not included or incorrectly attributed is asked to contact the publisher of this book so that correct credit can be made in the next printing.

Contents

Introduction

For almost 2,000 years the mysteries of Christianity have nourished the human spirit. They have been an incredible and almost inexhaustible treasury of wisdom and love, of inspiration and encouragement, of faith and hope.

Both the learned and the devout have found in this treasury a source that fed their minds, searching for truth, and their hearts, searching for the meaning of life.

The Incarnation of Jesus Christ, true God and true man, brought something into human history that meant a surge of hope for a world that knew only might and misery. The powerful, the proud, and the brave acted their parts in history and then were swallowed up in death. The poor and the downtrodden were, as usual, the anonymous characters in history.

Then Christ came into the world. He gave purpose to the strong and powerful, and He gave the promise of eternal life and love to all, from the mightiest to the lowliest.

But it was not a "magical" power. The Holy Spirit forms Christ in all who open themselves to His work. This means that we must cooperate with the graces of God to know and learn the message of Christ.

The grace that is freely given must find a human willingness to respond. The faith that cannot be merited must come alive with charity, with good works.

How is this done? That is a question that must be answered by each generation, by each individual. The answers of past ages show us the way in our turn.

In this book we will look at the answers that other centuries discovered for themselves, and we will share their insights. They applied the message of Christ to their own times, but they also went above their own times to offer applications that we can appreciate. They brought the understanding of men and women under pressures that we can only appreciate historically.

Time itself is only another creation of God's, and those historically close to Christ, say in the first three or four centuries, had no corner on the timeless application of the Christian challenge. Every century transcends time when it comes to Christ. He is the eternal "now" for all Christians.

The growth and development of Christianity, under the continual guidance of the Holy Spirit, is a dynamic event, at home in every period and place. The *magisterium*, the living voice of the Church, is able to apply Christ to everyone.

We do not have a dead faith or a faith in a past book, no matter how sacred that book. We have a living faith that is at home in the past, the present, and the future. As long as time endures, as long as this human race lives, the Catholic Church will be able to address the needs and desires of all people. If, as seems possible, we move out into space, the Church will be just as modern and just a little more ancient. The "ever ancient, ever new" of St. Augustine.

This book is a primer, a sampler, of the wisdom of the ages that the Catholic Church always presents to its members. It is an invitation to study Christ and make Him your own personal friend, through the friends He has made throughout history.

It is my hope that you will enjoy these excerpts and that you will then go to your own favorite authors and follow them more thoroughly as they gazed into the eternal depths of Jesus Christ.

[1]
The Post-Apostolic Age

The Catholic Book of Wisdom, *par excellence*, is the Bible. The Catholic Church is the Mother and Interpreter of the Bible, and guarantees its authenticity and content.

In the decades and centuries immediately following the death of the last Apostle, St. John, there was no Bible as we know it. There was great and widespread confusion as to what books were actually inspired, and what parts. Many apocryphal gospels and epistles were in circulation.

It was not until the fifth century, thanks to the work of Pope St. Damasus and St. Jerome, that the Bible as we know it emerged and was officially proclaimed for the whole Catholic world. Damasus "canonized" the Sacred Scriptures as the Books that were accepted and used by the Church of Rome, in all their parts. No more; no less.

So, the crisis that immediately faced the Christian Church at the start of the second century was how to preserve their apostolicity and what was to be the rule of faith when errors threatened.

It was a persecuted Church, since the Roman law stated it very simply: *Christiani non sint . . .* "There may be no Christians!" The great persecutions shed enough blood, and that blood was, indeed, the seed of Christians. But, to accept baptism, and thereby to become a Christian, meant the constant threat of death. To become a pope or a bishop meant almost certain death; few of them escaped martyrdom before A.D. 300.

From the precious writings and monuments that remain from the second and third centuries, several facts quickly emerge.

3

First, the organization of the Church, as left by the
Apostles, is historically demonstrated to be a hierarchical
church, with one bishop, several priests, and a group of
deacons established wherever there was a local church.

That was the visible form left by the Apostles to
guarantee that the Church would always be apostolic. These
clergymen had to be ordained by very strict rules to insure
the validity of the passing of priestly character.

For the most part, the rule of faith for the faithful
Christian was the role of faith taught by the local bishop.

And who was the chief bishop? There was never any
question, argument, or even discussion. It was the successor
of the Apostle St. Peter. The Bishop of Rome was not the first
among equals. He was simply the first, the head. All other
prerogatives or honors that grew during subsequent
centuries simply flowed from this theological and historic
fact.

This wasn't seriously questioned for a thousand years,
until the truly tragic Great Schism between the Eastern and
Western Churches. When the Protestant Reformers came on
the scene with their completely innovative and strange
interpretation of doctrine, they had to ignore the testimony
of the Fathers of the Church, or to read them very
selectively. History is simply not kind to the doctrine of the
Orthodox or the Protestants in this matter.

History is not ecumenical on the subject of the papacy.
The human side of the Church is constantly subject to
reform, as history also proves, but the divine element is a
constant.

Another interesting facet that comes through in these
times of persecution was the central place that the Eucharist
held in the life of the Church and the faithful. Despite the
disciplina arcani (Discipline of the Secret), the attempt to keep
the doctrine of the Real Presence of Christ in the Eucharist so
sacred and reserved that only the fully trained catechumen
might come to study it and receive it, there is eloquent

testimony from this period as to the tremendous importance of this sacrament.

The first term paper I ever wrote was on the writings of St. Ignatius of Antioch. Ever since my college days, therefore, he has been one of my favorites, but this section will also have samples of the works of such great minds as St. Justin Martyr, St. Irenaeus, and St. Cyprian. Origen and Tertullian also offer some interesting thoughts.

The Diognetus writings occur as an anonymous piece and also among the works attributed to St. Justin. To be on the safe side, I've included both opinions.

To set the context of this section, we see the Roman Empire surging past its prime and imperial politics of this time becoming increasingly sad. The petty kingdoms of the Goths and Visigoths were being set up and grew in strength as Rome declined.

Ptolemy and Galen were the scientists of the age, and in Alexandria, Diophantus produced the first book on algebra. Unknown to the people in the Mediterranean world, Buddhism was becoming the prominent religion in China and the Mayan civilization was growing in the western hemisphere.

¶1 • **Clement I, Pope St. †97** • **Letter to the Corinthians, No. 30** • Let us fix our attention on the blood of Christ and recognize how precious it is to God His Father, since it was shed for our salvation and brought the gift of repentance to all the world. . . .

Share then in the heritage of so many vast and glorious achievements; hasten toward the goal of peace, set before us from the very beginning. Keep your eyes firmly fixed on the Father and Creator of the whole universe and hold fast to His splendid and transcendent gifts of peace and all His blessings.

¶2 • _____ • **Letter to the Corinthians, No. 34** • We are not justified by our wisdom, intelligence, piety, or any action of ours, however holy, but by faith, the one means by which God has justified man from the beginning.

Then must we give up good works? Stop practicing Christian love? God forbid! We must be eager and ready for every opportunity to do good and to put our whole heart into it. Even the Creator and Lord of the universe rejoices in His good works.

All upright men have been graced in good works, and even the Lord Himself takes delight in the glory His works give Him.

¶3 • _____ • **Letter to the Corinthians, No. 35** • This is the path by which we find our salvation, Jesus Christ, the High Priest of our sacrifice, the defender and ally in our helplessness.

It is through Him that we gaze on the highest heaven, through Him we can see the reflection of God's pure and sublime countenance, through Him the eyes of our hearts have been opened, through Him our foolish and darkened understanding opens toward the light, and through Him God has willed that we should taste everlasting knowledge.

¶4 • _____ • **Letter to the Corinthians, No. 36** • Jesus Christ is our salvation. He is the High Priest through whom we present our offerings and the helper who supports us in our weakness. Through Him our gaze penetrates the heights of heaven and we see, as in a mirror, the most holy face of God. Through Christ the eyes of our hearts are opened and our weak and clouded understanding reaches up toward the light.

Let us, then, preserve the unity of the body that we form in Jesus Christ. . . .

¶5 • _____ **• Letter to the Corinthians, Concl. •** Lord, You
created the world according to the eternal decree now
revealed in Your works. Faithful through all generations,
You are just in judgment, wonderful in power and majesty.
You formed Your creation with wisdom and established it
with prudence. Everything we see proclaims Your goodness.
You are kind and compassionate and never fail those who put
their trust in You. . . . Forgive us for our failings and our
sins.

¶6 • Ignatius of Antioch, St. †c. 110 • Letter to Polycarp, No. 1 •
Justify your episcopal dignity by your unceasing concern for
the spiritual and temporal welfare of your flock. Let unity,
the greatest of all good, be your preoccupation. Carry the
burdens of all men as the Lord carries yours. Have patience
with all in charity, as indeed you do.

Give yourself to prayer continually, ask for wisdom
greater than you now have, keep alert with an unflagging
spirit. Speak to each man individually following God's
example, like a perfect athlete. The greater the toil, the richer
the reward.

¶7 • _____ **• Letter to Polycarp, No. 6 •** Pay attention to the
bishop, if you would have God pay attention to you. I offer
myself up for those who obey the bishop, priests and
deacons. . . .

Let your baptism be ever your shield, your faith a helmet,
your charity a spear, your patience a panoply. Let your
works be deposits, so that you may receive the sum that is
due you. In humility be patient with one another, as God is
with you.

¶8 • _____ **• Letter to the Ephesians, No. 2 •** It is right for you
to give glory in every way to Jesus Christ who has given
glory to you. You must be made holy in all things by being

united in perfect obedience, in submission to the bishop and the priests.

¶9 • _____ • **Letter to the Magnesians, No. 6** • Those who lived by the ancient customs attained a fresh hope; they no longer observed Saturday, but Sunday, the Lord's Day, for on that day life arose for us through Christ and through His death. Through this mystery we have received our faith and because of it we persevere, that we may prove to be disciples of our only teacher Jesus Christ.

¶10 • _____ • **Letter to the Philadelphians, No. 3** • Be careful, therefore, to take part in the one Eucharist, for there is only one Flesh of our Lord Jesus Christ, and one cup to unite us with His Blood, one altar and one bishop with the priests and deacons who are his fellow servants. Then, whatever you do you will do according to God. . . . As sons of the light of truth, flee divisions and evil doctrines.

¶11 • _____ • **Letter to the Romans, No. 3** • Let me be the food of beasts that I may come to God. I am His wheat, and I shall be ground by the teeth of beasts, that I may become Christ's pure bread. . . .

The fire, the cross, packs of wild beasts, lacerations, rendings, wrenching of bones, mangling of limbs, crunching of the whole body, the horrible tortures of the devil — let all these things come upon me, if only I may gain Jesus Christ!

¶12 • _____ • **Letter to the Smyrnaeans, No. 3** • By His resurrection, Christ raised up a standard over His saints and faithful ones for all time, both Jews and Gentiles, in the one body of His Church. For He endured all this for us, for our salvation; He really suffered and just as truly rose from the dead.

As for myself, I am convinced that He was united with His body even after the Resurrection.

¶ 13 • _____ • **Letter to the Trallians, No. 2** • All should respect deacons as Jesus Christ, just as all should regard the bishop as the image of the Father and the clergy as God's senate and the college of the apostles. Without these three orders you cannot begin to speak of a church.

Do nothing without your bishop and, indeed, be subject to the clergy as well, seeing in them the apostles of Jesus Christ our hope, for if we live in Him we shall be found in Him.

¶ 14 • **Polycarp, St. †c. 110** • **Letter to the Philippians, No. 5** • Priests should be sympathetic and merciful to everyone, bringing back those who have wandered, visiting the sick and the poor. Deacons, in the same way must be blameless in the sight of God.

Be steadfast, then, and follow the Lord's example, strong and unshaken in faith, loving the community as you love one another. United in the truth, show the Lord's own gentleness in your dealings with one another, and look down on no one. If you can do good, do not put it off, because almsgiving frees one from death.

¶ 15 • _____ • **On Martyrdom, Nos. 17, 18** • We worship Christ as the Son of God, while we love the martyrs as disciples and imitators of the Lord, for their insuperable affection for their own King and Teacher. With them may we also be made companions and fellow-disciples. . . .

Afterwards, we took up his bones, more valuable than precious stones and finer than gold, and put them in a proper place. There, as far as we are able, the Lord will permit us to meet together in gladness and joy and to celebrate the birthday of his martyrdom, both in memory of those who fought the fight and for the training and preparation of those who will fight.

¶16 • **Alexander I, Pope St. †115** • Among sacrifices there can be none greater than the Body and Blood of Christ, nor any more powerful oblation.

¶17 • **Sixtus I, Pope St. †125** • **The Ring, passim** • The man without faith is a living corpse. . . . God is not the name of God, but an opinion about Him. . . . God does not listen to the prayers of the lazy. . . . The chief aim of wisdom is to enable one to bear with the stupidity of the ignorant.

¶18 • **Barnabas* †c. 125** • **Epistle, Ch. 1** • The Lord has given us three basic doctrines: hope for eternal life, the beginning and end of our faith; justice, the beginning and end of righteousness; and love, which bears cheerful and joyful witness to the works of righteousness. [*This is an anonymous tract from the early second century.]

¶19 • **Aristotle †c. 137** • **Apology, Ch. 15** • Christians have the commandments of the Lord Jesus Christ himself engraved on their hearts, and these they observe, looking for the resurrection of the dead and the life of the world to come. . . . They do not do unto others that which they would not have done to themselves.

¶20 • **The Didache (2nd cent.), Ch. 7** • Regarding baptism, baptize in this way. After giving the instructions, baptize "in the name of the Father, and of the Son, and of the Holy Spirit" in running water. If you have no running water, baptize in any other, and if you cannot in cold water, then in warm.
But if one is lacking, pour the other three times on the head "in the name of the Father, and Son, and Holy Spirit."

¶21 • _____ • **Ch. 14** • And on the Lord's Day, after you have come together, break bread and offer the Eucharist, having first confessed your sins, so that your sacrifice may be pure.

¶22 • _____ • **Ch. 15** • Elect, therefore, for yourselves, bishops and deacons worthy of the Lord, humble men and not covetous, and faithful and well-rested; for they also serve you in the ministry of the prophets and teachers.

¶23 • **Anon. †150** • **Letter to Diognetus, No. 8** • God, the Lord and Creator of all, who made all things and set them in order, was not merely a lover of mankind, but was full of compassion. Mild and good, calm and true, He always was and is and will be; He alone is good. . . .

The great and ineffable Idea which He conceived He communicated to His Son alone. . . . When, through His beloved Son He removed the veil and revealed what He had prepared for the beginning, He gave us all at once, participation in His gifts, the graces of being able to see and understand things beyond all our expectations.

¶24 • _____ • **Letter to Diognetus, No. 9** • What the soul is to the body, Christians are to the world.

¶25 • **Hermas †150** • **Shepherd, 2nd Parable** • The rich man has great wealth, but, so far as the Lord is concerned, he is poor, because he is distracted by his wealth. His confession, his prayer to the Lord, is very limited; that which he makes is insignificant and weak and has no power above.

So, when a rich man goes up to a poor man and helps him in his needs, he has the assurance that what he does for the poor man can procure a reward from God, for the poor man is rich in his power of intercession with God and in his confession.

¶26 • **Papias, St.* †c. 125** • Whenever anyone came my way who had been a follower of my seniors, I would ask for the

accounts of our seniors: What did Andrew or Peter say? Or
Philip or Thomas or James or John or Matthew, or any of the
Lord's disciples? . . . For as I see it, it is not so much from
books as from the living and permanent voice that I must
draw profit. [*As reported by Eusebius in his *History*, 3:39.]

¶27 • **Athenagoras (2nd cent.)** • **A Plea for the Christians, Ch. 9** • [The
prophets], lifted in ecstasy above the natural operations of
their minds by the impulse of the Divine Spirit, uttered the
things with which they were inspired, the Spirit making use
of them as a flute-player breathes into a flute.

¶28 • **Justin Martyr, St. (100 - 165)** • **First Apology, No. 33** • Isaiah
foretold, "Behold a virgin shall conceive and bear a son and
His name shall be called Emmanuel" (i.e., God with us). For
what man has deemed incredible and impossible, God
foretold through the prophetic spirit.

The words mean that the virgin shall conceive without
intercourse. For if she had had intercourse with anyone
whomsoever, she was no longer a virgin, but the power of
God descending upon the virgin overshadowed her and
caused her, while still a virgin, to conceive.

¶29 • _____ • **First Apology, No. 66** • No one may share the
Eucharist with us unless he believes that what we teach is
true, unless he is washed in the regenerating waters of
baptism for the remission of sins, and unless he lives in
accordance with the principles given us by Christ. . . .

We hold our common assembly on Sunday because it is
the first day of the week, because on that day our Savior,
Jesus Christ, rose from the dead.

¶30 • _____ • **Letter No. 2*** • No man has ever seen God
or known Him, but God has revealed Himself to us through
faith, by which alone it is possible to see Him. God, the Lord

and maker of all things, who created the world and set it in
order, not only loved man but was patient with him.

So He has always been, and is, and will ever be: kind,
good, free from anger, truthful — indeed, He and He alone is
good. [*Some scholars consider this an anonymous letter
from a mid-second-century author.]

¶31 • _____ • **Letter to Diognetus,* No. 5** • Christians are
indistinguishable from other men either by nationality,
language, or customs. They do not inhabit separate cities of
their own or speak a strange dialect or follow some
outlandish way of life. . . .

And yet there is something extraordinary about their
lives. They live in their own countries as though they were
only passing through. They play their full role as citizens but
labor under all the disabilities of aliens. . . .

To speak in general terms, the Christian is to the world
what the soul is to the body. [*See ¶ 23, 24.]

¶32 • **Tatian †c. 165** • **Oration against the Greeks, Ch. 5** • God was
in the beginning; but the beginning, we have been taught, is
the power of the *Logos*. For the Lord of the universe, who is
himself the necessary ground of all being, inasmuch as no
creature was yet in existence, was alone; the *Logos* subsists
in Him. . . .

¶33 • **Dionysius of Corinth, St. †c. 171** • **Letter to the Romans** • In
these ways you also, by such an admonition, have united the
planting that came from Peter and Paul, or both of Romans
and the Corinthians. For indeed, both planted also in our
Corinth, and likewise taught us; and likewise they taught
together also in Italy and were martyred at the same time.

¶34 • **Theophilus of Antioch, St. †180** • **To Autolycus, 1:12** • Are
you willing to be anointed with the oil of God? We are called

Christians on this account, because we are anointed with the oil of God.

¶35 • _____ • **To Autolycus, 2:25** • So also for the first man, disobedience procured his expulsion from Paradise. It was not as if there were any evil in the tree of knowledge, but from his disobedience did man draw, as from a fountain, labor, pain, grief, and at last fall a prey to death.

¶36 • **Origen (185 - 253)** • **Dialogue with Heraclides** • We affirm that God is the almighty, God without beginning, without end, containing all things and not contained by anything. His Word is the Son of God, God and man, through whom all things were made, God according to the spirit, man inasmuch as He was born of Mary.

¶37 • _____ • **On First Principles, Bk. 4, Ch. 2** • We must point out that the aim of the Spirit who, by the providence of God through the Word who was "in the beginning with God," enlightened the servants of the truth, that is, the prophets and apostles, was preeminently concerned with the unspeakable mysteries connected with the affairs of men — and by men I mean at the present moment souls that make use of bodies — His purpose being that the man who is capable of being taught might, by "searching out" and devoting himself to the "deep things" revealed in the spiritual meaning of the words, become partaker of all the doctrines of the Spirit's counsel.

¶38 • **Irenaeus, St. (120 - 203)** • **Against Heresies, Bk. 3, No. 3** • The seduction of a fallen angel drew Eve, a virgin soon to be united to her husband, while the glad tidings of the holy angel drew Mary, a virgin already espoused, to begin the plan which would dissolve the bonds of the first snare. . . .
    The Virgin Mary has become the advocate for the Virgin

Eve. Death was brought upon the world by a virgin; life has triumphed by the Virgin Mary's obedience, which has finally balanced the debt of disobedience.

¶ 39 • _____ • **Against Heresies, Bk. 4, No. 6** • To believe in God means to do His will.

¶ 40 • _____ • **Against Heresies, Bk. 4, No. 17** • Our Lord instructed His disciples to offer to God the first-fruits of creation, not because God has any needs, but so that they themselves should not be unproductive and ungrateful. That is why He took bread, a part of His creation, gave thanks and said, "This is My Body." In the same way He declared that the cup, an element of the same creation as ourselves, was His Blood. He taught them that this was the new sacrifice of the new covenant. The Church has received this sacrifice from the apostles.

¶ 41 • _____ • **Against Heresies, Bk. 4, No. 20** • There is one God who by His word and wisdom created all things and set them in order. His Word is Our Lord Jesus Christ, who in this last age became man among men to unite end and beginning, that is, man and God.

¶ 42 • _____ • **Against Heresies, Bk. 4, No. 21** • Life in man is the glory of God; the life of man is the vision of God.

¶ 43 • _____ • **Against Heresies, Bk. 5, No. 20** • That is why the Lord proclaims himself "Son of Man," the one who renews in himself that first man from whom the race born of woman was formed; as by a man's defeat our race fell into the bondage of death, so by a man's victory we were to rise to life again.

¶ 44 • _____ • **Against Heresies, Bk. 5, No. 2** • Our bodies, which have been nourished by the Eucharist, will be buried in the earth and will decay, but they will rise again at the appointed time, for the Word of God will raise them up to the glory of God the Father. Then the Father will clothe our mortal nature in immortality and freely endow our corruptible nature with incorruptibility, for God's power is shown most perfectly in weakness.

¶45 • _____ • **Against Heresies, Bk. 6, No. 20** • The glory of God is man fully alive; and the life of man is the vision of God.

¶46 • **Clement of Alexandria, St. (c. 150 - 215)** • **Christ the Educator, Bk. 1, No. 12** • We are educated not for war but for peace. In war there is need for much equipment, just as self-indulgence craves abundance. But peace and love, simple and plain blood sisters, do not need arms or abundant supplies.

Their nourishment is the Word, the Word whose leadership enlightens and educates, from whom we learn poverty and humility and all that goes with love of freedom and of mankind and of the good. Simply, through Him we become like God by a likeness of virtue.

¶47 • _____ • **On the Rich Man** • Riches which benefit our neighbors are not to be thrown away. They are possessions and goods inasmuch as they are useful and provided by God for the use of men.

The Lord so enjoins the use of property as to add that it be shared, that the thirsty be given drink, the hungry bread, the naked clothes, and the homeless shelter. It is not possible to supply these needs without substance.

¶48 • **Tertullian †c. 220** • **Apology, 9:8** • For us, murder is once and for all forbidden; so even the child in the womb, while yet the mother's blood is still being drawn on to form the human being, it is not lawful for us to destroy. To forbid birth is only to murder the sooner.

It makes no difference whether one takes away the life

once born or destroys it as it comes to birth. He is a man who is to be a man; the fruit is always present in the seed.

¶49 • _____ • **Apology, 39:7** • "See," they say, "how those Christians love one another," while they themselves hate one another;

"And how they are ready to die for one another," while they themselves are ready to kill one another.

¶50 • _____ • **Letter to Scapula, No. 2** • It is the law of mankind and the natural right of each individual to worship what he thinks proper, nor does the religion of one man either help or hinder another. But it is not proper for religion to compel men to religion, which should be accepted on one's own accord, not by force.

¶51 • _____ • **On Baptism, No. 16** • There is to us one, and but one, Baptism; as well according to the Lord's Gospel as according to the Apostle's letters.

¶52 • **Hippolytus, St. (170 - 235)** • **Apostolic Tradition, Pt. 1** • Let the bishop be ordained after he has been chosen by all the people. When he has been named and shall please all, let him, with the priests and such bishops as may be present, assemble with the people on Sunday.

While all give their consent, the bishops shall lay their hands upon him, and the priests shall stand by in silence. All, indeed, shall keep silent, praying in their hearts for the descent of the Spirit. Then one of the bishops present shall, at the request of all, lay his hand on him who is ordained and shall pray. . . .

¶53 • _____ • **On the Refutation of Heresies, Ch. 10** • Our faith is not founded on empty words, nor are we carried away by mere caprice or beguiled by specious arguments. We put our faith in words spoken by the power of God, spoken by the Word himself at God's commands.

God wished to win man back from disobedience, not by using force to reduce him to slavery, but by addressing a call to liberty to his free will.

¶ 54 • **Minucius Felix †c. 250** • **Letter to Octavius, No. 18** • By His Word, God calls into existence all things that are, disposes them according to His wisdom, and perfects them by His goodness. God is invisible, because too bright for our sight; intangible, because too fine for our senses to touch; immeasurable, because He is beyond the grasp of our senses; infinite, limitless, His real magnitude known to Himself alone.

¶ 55 • _____ • **Letter to Octavius, No. 34** • The whole body, whether it withers away to dust, or dissolves into moisture, or crumbles away to ashes, or passes off in vapor, is removed from our eyes, but it still exists for God, the Preserver of the elements. Nor are we, as you imagine, afraid of any damage resulting from the manner of burial, but we practice the time-honored and more dignified custom of consigning the dead body to the earth.

I know perfectly well, of course, that many, because of their guilty conscience, hope rather than believe that they are reduced to nothing after death. They prefer to be annihilated rather than be restored for punishment.

¶ 56 • **Firmilian (3rd cent.)** • **Letter to Cyprian** • But what of the greatness of the error, and what the depth of the blindness of one who says that remission of sins can be granted in the synagogues of heretics, and does not abide on the foundation of the one Church which was one based on Christ upon the Rock, may be perceived from this, that the power of remitting sins was given to the Apostles, and to the churches which they, sent by Christ, established, and to the bishops who succeeded them by vicarious ordination.

¶57 • Stephen I, Pope St. †257 • Letter to Cyprian • Let them innovate in nothing, but keep the traditions. *(Nihil innovetur nisi quod traditum est.)*

¶58 • Cyprian, St. (200 - 258) • On Patience, Ch. 15 • Charity is the bond of brotherhood, the foundation of peace, the steadfastness and firmness of unity; it is greater than both faith and hope; it surpasses both good works and suffering for the faith; and, as an external virtue, it will abide with us forever in the kingdom of heaven.

Take patience away from it, and thus forsaken, it will not last; take away the substance of enduring and tolerating, and it attempts to last without roots or strength.

¶59 • _____ • On the Lord's Prayer • The Lord has given us many counsels and commandments to help us toward salvation. He has even given us a pattern of prayer, instructing us on how we are to pray. He has given us life, and, with His accustomed generosity, He has also taught us how to pray.

He has made it easy for us to be heard as we pray to the Father in the words taught us by the Son. . . . What more effective prayer could we make in the name of Christ than in the words of His own prayer?

¶60 • _____ • The Unity of the Church, No. 6 • He cannot have God as a Father who does not have the Church as a mother.

He who breaks the peace and concord of Christ acts against Christ; he who gathers somewhere outside the Church scatters the Church of Christ.

He cannot possess the garment of Christ who tears and divides the Church of Christ.

¶61 • _____ • **On the Virtue of Patience** • Dear Brethren, we must endure and persevere if we are to attain the truth and freedom we have been allowed to hope for. Faith and hope are the very meaning of our being Christians, but if faith and hope are to bear fruit, patience is necessary. . . .

Neither unity nor peace can be maintained unless the brethren cherish each other with mutual forbearance and preserve the bond of harmony by means of patience.

¶62 • **Novatian (c. 200 - 258)** • **The Trinity, Ch. 11.** • Therefore, let those who read in the Scripture that the man, Christ Jesus, is the Son of Man, also read there that this same Jesus is called both God and the Son of God.

In the same manner that He, as man, is of Abraham, even so, as God, is He also before Abraham himself.

In the same manner that He, as man, is the Son of David, so is He also, as God, called the Lord of David.

¶63 • **Dionysius of Alexandria, St. †265** • **Elenchus, No. 1** • There certainly was never a time when God was not the Father. The Son, being the brightness of eternal light, He Himself is absolutely eternal. . . . Since, therefore, the Father is eternal, the Son is also eternal, light of light.

For where there is the begetter there is also the offspring. If there were no offspring, how and of what could He be the begetter? But, both are, and always are.

¶64 • _____ • **Letter to Novatian** • For this a man ought to suffer anything and everything, rather than divide the Church of God, and it is no less glorious to incur martyrdom to avoid schism than to avoid idolatry; in fact, in my opinion, it is more so. For in the one case a man is a martyr for the sake of his own single soul, but in the other for the sake of the whole Church.

¶ 65 • **Gregory Thaumaturgus, St. †270** • **Profession of Faith, No. 1** •
There is one God, the Father of the living Word, who is His
subsistent Wisdom and Power and eternal Image: perfect
begetter of the perfect begotten, Father of the only-begotten
Son.

There is one Lord, Only of the Only, God of God, Image
and Likeness of Deity, Efficient Word, Wisdom
comprehensive of the constitution of all things, and Power
formative of the whole creation, true Son of true Father,
Invisible of Invisible, and Incorruptible of Incorruptible, and
Immortal of Immortal, and Eternal of Eternal. . . .

And there is one Holy Spirit, having His subsistence from
God and being made manifest to men by the Son, Perfect
Image of the Perfect, Life, the Cause of Living, Holy Fount,
Sanctity. . . .

[2]
The Age of the Fathers

As the Church entered its fourth century, the Edict of Milan by the Emperor Constantine the Great granted legal rights to the Christians of the Roman Empire, and a great feeling of peace and good will swept over all. Except for a brief and bitter struggle under the Emperor Julian the Apostate, the Catholic Church became the dominant religious force.

However, the persecutions from without were nowhere near as bitter as the blows from within, the heresies that sprang up almost immediately. As the glorious martyrs proved the front line of defense before, now the heroes were the great theologians who were raised up to defend the true Faith.

In the Eastern or Oriental Church (along the eastern side of the Mediterraneaon world) the names that come quickly to mind are the Gregorys, Basil, John Chrysostom, the Cyrils, and Athanasius.

When John Henry Newman pondered the works of St. Athanasius, he asked himself if Athanasius would recognize the Church of England as a truly Catholic church. As he was forced to conclude that Athanasius would not accept his Church, Newman pondered over what Church would be acceptable. The only answer he could come up with was the Church of Rome. Forced by this logic, Newman became a Roman Catholic and one of the intellectual giants in the Church of his generation.

St. Gregory of Nazianzus was considered so brilliant a theologian that he was frequently referred to simply as "the theologian" — *theologus*. The only other intellectual I know of who was accorded such honor is Aristotle, who is usually

23

referred to as "the philosopher" — *philosophus.*

In the Western Church there lived Hilary of Poitiers, Ambrose of Milan, Jerome, Leo the Great, and, without a doubt, the giant of this Age of the Fathers, St. Augustine. His conversion, sixteen hundred years ago, changed the direction of Christianity as surely as did the conversion of St. Paul on the road to Damascus.

If I had to choose the three most influential saints in the history of Christianity, after the Apostolic Age, I would have no hesitation in picking St. Augustine, St. Thomas Aquinas, and St. Bernard, in that order.

This particular time also saw the convening of at least five great ecumenical councils. Nicaea I was called by Pope St. Sylvester in 325 to condemn Arianism. In Constantinople in 381, Pope St. Damasus I called together a council which continued the work of Nicaea. At Ephesus in 431, Pope St. Celestine I convoked the meeting to condemn Nestorianism and proclaim the divinity of Christ with the famous word *Theotokos* (God-bearer) that declared Mary, formally, the Mother of God.

The Council of Chalcedon defended the humanity of Christ in its sessions in 451, and then it was back to Constantinople in 553, again to condemn Nestorianism. There was vigorous theological activity that went into the need for such councils, and each one contributed to the arguments for the next.

In the secular context of these things, the Roman Empire was dying, slowly and painfully, and gradually the legions had to be withdrawn from the frontiers to protect Italy. The inroads by the barbarians became increasingly more widespread, ugly, and fierce.

Mayan and Inca artifacts from these centuries became more abundant, and the first provable history of Japan comes from this time.

Church music came to prominence in Europe in these years, and many of the great basilicas of Rome were started.

¶66 • Lactantius (c. 240 - 320) • The Divine Institutes, Bk. 5, Ch. 8 •
For if God alone were worshiped, there would not be
dissensions and wars. When men would know that they are
sons of the one God, and therefore bound together by a
sacred, inviolable bond of divine relationship, no insidious
plots would take place.

When they knew what sort of punishments God was
preparing for the killers of souls, the God who sees through
clandestine crimes and even thoughts themselves, there
would not be frauds and rapine.

¶67 • _____ • The Divine Institutes, Bk. 5, Ch. 14 • Piety is
nothing other than getting acquainted with God.

**¶68 • Eusebius of Caesarea (c. 260 - c. 339) • Ecclesiastical History,
Bk. 3 •** While Ignatius of Antioch was making his journey
through Asia under the strictest military guard, he
strengthened the diocese in each city where he stayed by oral
sermons and exhortations, and he especially exhorted them
above all to be on guard against the heresies which then for
the first time were prevalent, and he urged them to hold fast
to the tradition of the Apostles to which he thought it
necessary, for security's sake, to give form to written
testimony.

¶69 • _____ • Ecclesiastical History, Bk. 10 • [When
Constantine granted peace to the Church] our bishops
performed religious rites with full ceremonial, priests
officiated at the liturgy — the solemn ritual of the Church,
chanting psalms, proclaiming the other parts of the God-
given Scriptures, and celebrating the divine mysteries.
Baptism was also administered, the sacred symbol of the
Savior's passion.

¶70 • Aphraates, †c. 350 • Demonstrations, 8:3 • Each of the
seeds is clothed in its own body. Never do you sow wheat

and reap barley; never do you plant a vine and it produces figs; but everything grows according to its own nature.

Thus also, the body which was laid in the earth is that which shall rise again. And as to this, that the body is corrupted and wastes away, you ought to be instructed by the parable of the seed, that as the seed, when it is cast into the earth, decays and is corrupted, and from its decay it produces and buds and bears fruit.

¶71 • **Arnobius the Elder (4th cent.)** • **Against the Heathen, Bk. 1, Ch. 42** • But since He [Christ] is God in reality and without any shadow of doubt, do you think that we will deny that He is worshiped by us with all the fervor we are capable of, and assumed as the guardian of our body?

Is that Christ of yours a god, then? some will ask. A god, we will reply, indeed *the* God of the inner powers.

¶72 • **Constitutions of the Apostles (c. 350)** • **8:28** • A bishop blesses, he is not blessed; he imposes hands, he ordains, he offers; he receives a blessing from bishops, but never from priests. . . .

A priest blesses, he is not blessed except by bishops; he imposes hands, he does not ordain. . .

A deacon does not bless. . . A deaconess does not bless, nor do any of the things which priests and deacons do; she alone minds the doors and ministers to priests when they baptize women, for decency's sake.

¶73 • _____ • **3:16** • The bishop shall anoint the head of those that are to be baptized, whether they are men or women, with the holy oil. . . . After that, either the bishop or his priest shall, in the solemn form, name over them the Father and the Son and the Holy Spirit and shall then immerse them in the water. . . . After that, let the bishop anoint those who are baptized with ointment.

¶74 • Epiphanius of Constantia, St. (4th cent). • Panarion, Against the Heretics, No. 73 • We confess the Father and the Son and the Holy Spirit to be consubstantial, three hypostases (persons), one essence, one divinity. That is the true faith handed down by the Fathers, and is prophetic and evangelical and apostolic, which our fathers and bishops have professed, who were gathered together in the Council of Nicaea when the great and blessed Constantine was Emperor.

¶75 • Pacianus of Barcelona, St. †360 • Letters 1:4 • Christian is my name and Catholic is my surname. The former qualifies me, the latter manifests me for what I am. And, if I finally must explain the word "Catholic" and translate it from the Greek into the Latin idiom, Catholic means "one everywhere" or, as the more learned think, "obedience to all the commandments of God."

¶76 • Hilary of Poitiers, St. (c. 315 - c. 368) • On the Trinity, Bk. 2 • God is invisible, ineffable, infinite. In speaking of Him in this fashion, even speech is silent; the mind becomes weary in trying to fathom Him; the understanding is limited in comprehending Him. . . . He himself is unborn, eternal, and always possesses in himself what He is. . . . It is the Father from whom everything that exists has being. He is in Christ and through Christ the source of all things.

¶77 • _____ • On the Holy Trinity, Bk. 8 • We believe that the Word became flesh and that we receive His flesh in the Lord's Supper. How then can we fail to believe that He really dwells within us? When He became man, He actually clothed himself in our flesh, uniting it to himself forever. In the Sacrament of His Body He actually gives us His own flesh, which He has united to His divinity. This is why we are all one, because the Father is in Christ and Christ is in us.

¶78 • Athanasius, St. (c. 297 - 373) • Letter to Adelphius, Ch. 3 •
We do not worship a creature. Far be the thought! Such an
error belongs to heathens and Arians. We worship the Lord
of creation, Incarnate, the Word of God. For if the flesh also is
in itself a part of the created world, yet it has become God's
Body. And we neither divide the body, being such, from the
Word and worship it by itself, nor when we wish to worship
the Word do we set Him apart from the flesh, but knowing, as
we said above, that "the Word was made flesh," we recognize
Him as God also, after having come in the flesh.

¶79 • _____ • Letter to Serapion, 1:28 • Consider the ancient
tradition, teaching, and faith of the Catholic Church which
was revealed by the Lord, proclaimed by the Apostles, and
guarded by the Fathers. . . .
We acknowledge the Trinity, holy and perfect, to consist
of the Father, the Son, and the Holy Spirit. In this Trinity
there is no intrusion of any alien element or of anything from
outside, nor is the Trinity a blend of creative and created
being.
It is a wholly creative and energizing reality, self-
consistent and undivided in its active power, for the Father
makes all things through the Word and in the Holy Spirit and
in this way the unity of the Holy Trinity is preserved.

¶80 • _____ • Letter 14 • In former times the blood of
goats and the ashes of a calf were sprinkled on those who
were unclean, but they were able to purify only the body.
Now through the grace of God's Word everyone is made
abundantly clean.
If we follow Christ closely, we shall be allowed, even on
this earth, to stand as it were on the threshold of the
heavenly Jerusalem, and enjoy the contemplation of the
everlasting feast, like the blessed Apostles, who in following
the Savior as their leader, showed, and still show, the way to
obtain the same gift from God.

¶81 • _____ • **Sermon on the Incarnation, No. 8** • This is the reason why the Word assumed a body that could die: this was the way in which the Word was to restore mankind to immortality, after it had fallen into corruption, and summon it back from death to life.

He utterly destroyed the power death had against mankind, as fire consumes chaff, by means of the body He had taken and the grace of the Resurrection.

¶82 • **Ephrem, St. †373** • **Third Sermon, No. 2** • In Your sacrament we daily embrace You and receive You into our bodies; make us worthy to experience the resurrection for which we hope. We have had Your treasure hidden within us ever since we received baptismal grace; it grows ever richer at Your sacramental table.

Teach us to find our joy in Your favor. Lord, we have within us Your memorial, received at Your spiritual table; let us possess it in its full reality when all things shall be made new.

¶83 • **Basil the Great, St. (c. 329 - c. 379)** • **Letter 188** • A woman who deliberately destroys a fetus is answerable for murder. And any fine distinction as to its being completely formed or unformed is not admissable among us.

¶84 • _____ • **Letter 261** • Accordingly, He took our flesh with its natural feelings but He "did no sin." Yet, even as death in the flesh, which was handed down to us through Adam, was swallowed up by the godhead, so also sin was utterly destroyed by the justice which is in Jesus Christ, so that in the resurrection we resume our flesh, which is neither liable to death nor subject to sin.

These are the "mysteries" of the Church; these are the traditions of the Fathers.

¶85 • _____ • **Rules for Monks, No. 2** • Love of God is not something that can be taught. We did not learn from someone else how to rejoice in light or want to live or to love our parents. It is the same with our love of God. As soon as the living creature comes to be, a power of reason is implanted in us like a seed, containing within it the ability and the need to love. . . .

This is the definition of sin: the misuse of powers given us by God for doing good, a use contrary to God's commandments. Virtue is the use of the same powers based on a good conscience in accordance with God's commands.

¶86 • _____ • **Sermon on Charity** • Man should be like the earth and bear fruit. He should not let inanimate matter appear to surpass him. The earth bears fruit for your benefit, not for its own, but when you give to the poor, you are bearing fruit which you will gather in for yourself, since the reward for good deeds goes to those who perform them. Give to a hungry man and what you give becomes yours, and indeed, it returns to you with interest.

As the sower profits from the wheat that falls onto the ground, so will you profit greatly in the world to come from the bread that you place before a hungry man. Your husbandry must be the sowing of heavenly seed.

¶87 • **Damasus I, Pope St. †384** • **Prayer to St. Andrew** • O great St. Andrew, your name, a token of beauty, foretells your splendor in the glory of your holy cross. The cross exalts you, the blessed cross loves you, the bitter cross prepares the joys of the light to come for you.

The mystery of the cross shines in you with a twofold beauty: for by the cross you vanquished insults and taught all mankind of the Divine Blood shed on the cross. Give fervor to our languid hearts and take us under your care, that by the victory of the cross we may reach our home in heaven. Amen.

¶ 88 • **Cyril of Jerusalem, St. c. 350 - 387 • Catechesis, No. 21 •**
When we were baptized into Christ and clothed ourselves in
Him, we were transformed into the likeness of the Son of
God. Having destined us to be His adopted sons, God gave us
a likeness to Christ in His glory, and living as we do in
communion with Christ, God's anointed, we ourselves are
rightly called "the anointed ones."

¶ 89 • _____ • **Catechesis, No. 22 •** Do not, then, regard the
eucharistic elements as ordinary bread and wine. They are in
fact the Body and Blood of the Lord, as He himself has
declared. Whatever your senses may tell you, be strong in
faith.
  You have been taught and are firmly convinced that what
looks and tastes like bread and wine is not bread and wine
but the Body and Blood of Christ.

¶ 90 • _____ • **Catechesis, No. 18 •** The Church is called
Catholic or universal because it has spread throughout the
entire world, from one end of the earth to the other. Again, it
is called Catholic because it reaches fully and unfailingly all
the doctrines which ought to be brought to men's knowledge,
whether concerned with visible or invisible things, with the
realities of heaven and the things on earth.
  Another reason for the name Catholic is that the Church
brings all classes of men into religious obedience, rulers and
subjects, the learned and the unlettered. Finally it deserves
the word Catholic because it heals and cures unrestrictedly
every type of sin and because it possesses within itself every
kind of virtue.

¶ 91 • _____ • **Catechesis, No. 23 •** Then, after the spiritual
sacrifice, the bloodless service is completed, over that
sacrifice of propitiation we entreat God for the common peace
of the Churches; for the welfare of the world, for kings; for
soldiers and allies; and for the afflicted: in a word, for all who

stand in need of succor, we all pray and offer this sacrifice.

In the same way, when we make our supplications for those who have fallen asleep, though they be sinners, we offer up Christ sacrificed for our sins, propitiating our merciful God for them as well as for ourselves.

¶92 • **Gregory Nazianzen, St. (c. 330 - c. 390)** • **Letter No. 171** • But cease not to pray and to plead for me when you draw down the Word by your word, when with a bloodless cutting you sever the Body and Blood of the Lord, using your voice for the sword.

¶93 • _____ • **Oration No. 30** • As far then as we can reach, "He who Is" and "God" are the special names for His Essence; and of these especially He who Is, not only because when He spoke to Moses on the Mount, and Moses asked Him what His Name was, this was what He called himself, bidding him to say to the people, "The I AM has sent me" (Ex. 3:14) but also because we find this Name is the more strictly appropriate. . . .

God always was and always is and always will be; or rather, God always IS, for was and will be are fragments of our time and of our changeable nature.

¶94 • _____ • **Sermon 45** • The very Son of God, older than the ages, the invisible, the incomprehensible, the incorporeal, the beginning of the beginning, the light of light, the fountain of life and immortality, the image of the archetype, the immovable seal, the perfect likeness, the definition and word of the Father — He it is who comes in His own image and takes our nature for the good of our nature, and unites Himself to an intelligent soul for the good of our souls, to purify like by like.

¶95 • **Gregory of Nyssa, St. †394** • **On Christian Perfection** • Paul teaches us the power of Christ's name when he calls Him the

power and wisdom of God, our peace, the unapproachable
light, where God dwells, our expiation and redemption, our
great High Priest, our pastoral sacrifice, our propitiation;
when he declares Him to be the radiance of God's glory, the
very pattern of His nature, the creator of all ages, our
spiritual food and drink, the cornerstone, the visible image of
the invisible God.

He goes on to speak of Him as the mighty God, the Head
of His Body the Church, the firstborn of the new creation,
and the Mediator between God and man, the only-begotten
Son crowned with glory and honor.

¶96 • _____ • **Sermon on the Resurrection** • The reign of life
has begun; the tyranny of death is ended. A new birth has
taken place, a new life has come, a new order of existence has
appeared, our very nature has been transformed. . . .

Faith is the womb that conceives this new life, baptism
the rebirth by which it is brought forth. The Church is its
nurse, her teachings are its milk, and the bread from heaven
is its food.

It is brought to maturity by the practice of virtue; it is
wedded to wisdom; it gives birth to hope. Its home is the
kingdom, its end not death but the blessed and everlasting
life prepared for us.

¶97 • _____ • **On the Song of Songs, No. 15** • When love has
entirely cast out fear, and fear has been transformed into
love, then the unity brought by our Savior will be fully
realized, for all men will be united with one another through
their union with the one Supreme Good.

¶98 • **Rufinus of Aquileia (345 - c. 400)** • **Commentary on the
Apostles' Creed, No 8** • This then is Christ Jesus, the only Son of
God, who is also our Lord. "Only" can be applied to Him both
as Son and as Lord. For Jesus Christ is "only" both as God's
authentic Son and as our sole Lord. All other sons of God,

though designated sons, have their title by the grace of adoption, not as a result of any natural relationship.

¶99 • **Ambrose, St. (c. 340 - 397)** • **Christo profusum sanguinem** • The martyrs' triumphs let us sing, / Their blood poured forth for Christ the King, / And while due hymns of praise we pay, / Our thankful hearts cast grief away.

The world its terrors urged in vain; / They recked not of the body's pain; / One step, and holy death made sure / The life that ever shall endure.

¶100 • _____ • **Letters, No. 2** • Happy is the man who has been able to cut out that root of vice, avarice. . . . What do superfluous riches profit in this world when they do not assist our birth or impede our dying. We are born into this world naked; we leave it without a cent; we are buried without our inheritance.

¶101 • _____ • **The Mysteries, Ch. 9** • The Lord Jesus himself declares, "This is my Body." Before the blessing of the heavenly words, another species is mentioned; after the consecration the body is signified. He himself speaks of His Blood. Before the consecration it is mentioned as something else; after the consecration it is called Blood. And you say, "Amen," that is, "It is true." What the mouth speaks, let the mind within confess; what words utter, let the heart feel.

¶102 • _____ • **Nunc sancte nobis Spiritus, vv. 1, 2** • Come Holy Spirit, who ever one / Art with the Father and the Son, / It is the hour our soul possess / With Your full flood of holiness.

Let heart and flesh and lips and mind / Sound forth our witness to mankind / And love light up our mortal frame, / Till others catch the living flame.

¶103 • _____ • **On Luke, No. 2** • See the humility! Note well the devotion. She who has been chosen to be the mother of the Lord calls herself His little servant-girl. She certainly does not become haughty over this promise of so exalted a position. By calling herself a handmaiden she does not take as a right what is freely given as a grace.

¶104 • _____ • **On Psalm 1** • In the Book of Psalms there is profit for all with healing power for our salvation. There is instruction from history, teaching from the law, prediction from prophecy, chastisement from denunciation, and persuasion from moral preaching. . . .

All with eyes to see can discover in it a complete gymnasium for the soul, a stadium for all virtues, equipped for every kind of exercise. It is for each to choose the kind he judges best to help him gain the prize.

¶105 • _____ • **On Psalm 36** • When we speak about wisdom, we are speaking of Christ. When we speak about virtue, we are speaking of Christ. When we speak about justice, we are speaking of Christ. When we speak about peace, we are speaking of Christ. When we speak about truth and life and redemption, we are speaking of Christ.

¶106 • _____ • **Second Letter** • The Church of the Lord is built upon the rock of the Apostles among so many dangers in the world; it therefore remains unmoved. The Church's foundation is unshakeable and firm against the assaults of the raging sea. Waves lash at the Church but do not shatter it.

Although the elements of the world constantly beat upon the Church with crashing sounds, the Church possesses the safest harbor of salvation for all in distress.

¶107 • _____ • **Splendor Paternae Gloriae, vv. 1, 2** • O Splendor of God's glory bright, / O You who bring light from

light, / O Light of Light, light's living spring, / A Day all days
illumining.

O You true Son, on us Your glance / Let fall in royal
radiance, / The Spirit's sanctifying beam / Upon our earthly
senses stream.

¶108 • **Siricius, Pope St. †399** • **Decretal Letter to Himerius, No. 10** •
Now the Lord Jesus, when He illumined us by His appearing,
declared in the Gospel that He had come to fulfill the law, not
abolish it. He desired that the Church, whose Bridegroom He
is, should have her visage shining with the spendor of
chastity, that in the Day of Judgment, when He comes again,
He may find her without spot or blemish, as He ordained by
His apostle.

Hence all of us priests are bound by the unbreakable law
of those instructions to subdue our hearts and bodies to
soberness and modesty from the day of our ordination, that
we may be wholly pleasing to our God in the sacrifices we
daily offer.

¶109 • **John Chrysostom, St. †407** • **In Praise of St. Paul, No. 2** •
Paul, more than anyone else, has shown us what man really
is, and in what our nobility consists, and of what virtue this
particular animal is capable. Each day he aimed ever higher;
each day he rose up with greater ardor and faced with new
eagerness the dangers that threatened him.

The most important thing of all to him, however, was that
he knew he was loved by Christ. Enjoying this love, he
considered himself happier than anyone else.

¶110 • _____ • **The Priesthood, Ch. 2, No. 1** • Why did God
not spare His only-begotten Son, but delivered Him up? That
He might reconcile to himself those who were His enemies
and make them His own people. Why did He shed His Blood?
To purchase those sheep which He entrusted to Peter and his
successors.

¶111 • _____ • **On Matthew, No. 50** • Of what use is it to weigh down Christ's table with golden cups, when He himself is dying of hunger? First, fill Him when He is hungry, and then use the means you have left to adorn His table. I am not forbidding such gifts; I am only demanding that along with such gifts, and before them, you give alms. He accepts the former, but He is much more pleased with the latter.

¶112 • _____ • **Sermon on Prayer, No. 6** • Prayer and conversation with God is a supreme good. It is a partnership and union with God. . . .

Prayer is the light of the spirit, true knowledge of God, mediating between God and man. . . .

Prayer stands before God as an honored ambassador; it gives joy to the spirit and peace to the heart.

¶113 • _____ • **Sermon on Temptation** • There are five paths of repentance: condemnation of our own sins, forgiveness of our neighbor's sins against us, prayer, almsgiving, and humility.

¶114 • **Asterius of Amasea, St. †c. 410** • **On the Chief Apostles** • The Savior confided to this man [St. Peter], as some special trust, the whole universal Church, after having asked him three times, "Do you love me?" And he received the world in charge, as one flock one shepherd, having heard, "Feed my lambs"; and the Lord gave, well nigh in His own stead, that most faithful disciple to the proselytes as a father and shepherd and instructor.

¶115 • **Gaudentius of Brescia, St. †c. 413** • **Sermon 2** • The heavenly sacrifice, instituted by Christ, is the most gracious legacy of His new covenant. On the night He was delivered up to be crucified, He left us this gift as a pledge of His abiding presence.

This sacrifice is our sustenance on the journey of life. By

it we are nourished and supported along the road of life until
we depart from this world and make our way to the Lord.

¶116 • ———— • **Treatise, No. 2** • Creator and Lord of all
things, whatever their nature, He brought forth bread from
the earth and changed it into His own Body. Not only had He
the power to do this, but He had promised it. And, as He had
changed water into wine, He also changed wine into His own
Blood.

¶117 • **Prudentius, (348 - c. 413)** • **Ales Dueu Nuntius, vv. 1, 4** • As
sounds the bird whose clarion gay / Sounds before the dawn
is gray, / Christ, who bring's the spirit's day, / Calls us, close
at hand.
  Break the sleep of death and time, / Forged by Adam's
ancient crime; / And the light of Eden's prime / To the world
restore.

¶118 • **Nicetas of Remesiana †c. 415** • **Te Deum, vv. 16-20** • You
did not abhor the Virgin's womb when You took human
nature to deliver man. / When You overcame the sting of
death, You opened to believers the kingdom of heaven. / You
sit at the right hand of the God in the glory of the
Father. / You, we believe, are the Judge to come. / We beg
You, therefore, to help Your servants whom You have
redeemed with Your own Precious Blood. . .

¶119 • **Innocent I, Pope St. †419** • **Letter to Decentius** • "If anyone
among you is sick, let him call the priests, and let them pray
over him, anointing him with oil in the name of the Lord, and
if he has sinned, He will forgive him" (James 5:14). There is
no doubt that this ought to be understood of the faithful who
are sick and who can be anointed with the holy oil of the
chrism when it is necessary for themselves or their families.

¶ 120 • **Jerome, St. (c. 340 - c. 420)** • **Letter to Pope Damasus, No. 2** •
If anything could sustain and support a wise man in this life
or help him to preserve his equanimity amid the conflicts of
the world, it is, I think, meditation on the knowledge of the
Bible.

¶ 121 • _____ • **Letter No. 146** • For what function,
excepting ordination, belongs to a bishop that does not also
belong to a priest?

¶ 122 • _____ • **On Joel** • Return to the Lord your God,
from whom you have been alienated by your sins. Do not
despair of His mercy, no matter how great your sins, for great
mercy will take away great sins.

The Lord is gracious and merciful and prefers the
conversion of the sinner rather than his death. Patient and
generous in His mercy. He does not give in to human
impatience, but is willing to wait a long time for our
repentance. . . .

However, do not let the magnitude of His clemency make
us lax in repentance.

¶ 123 • _____ • **On the Assumption** • When the angel cried,
"Hail, full of grace, the Lord is with you; you are blessed
among women!" he told us by divine command how
tremendous was the dignity and beauty of the ever-virgin
Mary.

How well we can understand that she would be "full of
grace," this virgin who glorified God and gave Our Lord to
mankind, who poured out peace upon the earth by giving
hope to the gentiles, protection against temptation, purpose
of life and reason for sacrifice.

¶ 124 • **Boniface I, Pope St. †422** • **Letter 14** • The universal
ordering of the Church at its birth took its origin from the
office of blessed Peter, in which is found both its directing

power and its supreme authority. From him as from its source when our religion was in its growth stage, all the churches received their common order. This much is shown by the Council of Nicaea . . . which knew that all had been assigned to him by the word of the Lord.

So it is clear that this church is to all the churches throughout the world as the head is to the members, and that whoever separates himself from it becomes an exile from the Christian religion, since he ceases to belong to its fellowship.

¶125 • **Palladius of Helenopolis (c. 364 - c. 430)** • **Life of St. John Chrysostom, Ch. 20** • I would much prefer to travel the valleys and glens and the deep seas with truth than to possess great honor which the present world thinks of as prosperity and to be burdened the whole while with falsehood.

If I possess truth I shall possess all things, for all things serve truth. Should I possess falsehood, I am not my own master.

¶126 • **Augustine, St. (354 - 430)** • **Against the Errors of Faustus, No. 15** • These words from heaven, ringing above the banks of the river Jordan: "This is my beloved Son in whom I am well pleased." They were repeated on the mountain — not, of course, that He was not the Son of God before this pronouncement.

He took the form of a servant in the womb of the Virgin, even though He was by nature God. Equal to the Father, He did not think it wrong to claim their equality.

¶127 • _____ • **Against Faustus, Bk. 20** • We, the Christian community, assemble to celebrate the memory of the martyrs with ritual solemnity because we want to be inspired to follow their example, share in their merits, and be helped by their prayers. . . .

But the veneration strictly called worship, *latria*, that is,

the special homage belonging only to divinity, is something
we give and teach others to give to God alone.

¶128 • _____ • **The City of God, Bk. 10, No. 6** • Works of
mercy done either to ourselves or to our neighbor and
referred to God are true sacrifices. Works of mercy are
performed for no other reason than to free us from .
wretchedness and by this means to make us happy.

It clearly follows that the whole redeemed city, that is,
the assembly and fellowship of the saints, is offered to God as
a universal sacrifice through the great High Priest, who, in
the nature of a slave, offered himself for us in His passion, in
order that we might be the body of so great a Head.

¶129 • _____ • **Confessions, Bk. 9** • Thereupon she [St.
Monica] looked up at me and spoke: "Bury my body
wherever you will. Let not the care of it cause you any
concern. Only one thing I ask of you, that you remember me
at the altar of the Lord wherever you may be."

¶130 • _____ • **Confessions, Bk. 10** • Late have I loved You,
O Beauty ever ancient, ever new, late have I loved You.

You were within me, but I was outside, and it was there
that I searched for You. In my unloveliness I plunged into the
lovely things which You created. You were with me, but I
was not with You. Created things kept me from You; yet if
they had not been in You, they would not have been at all.

You called, You shouted, and You broke through my
deafness. You flashed, You shone, and You dispelled my
blindness. You breathed Your fragrance on me; I drew in
breath, and now I pant for You. I have tasted You and now I
hunger and thirst for more.

¶131 • _____ • **Confessions, Bk. 10** • O Lord, the depths of a
man's conscience lie exposed before Your eyes. Could
anything remain hidden in me, even though I did not want to

confess it to You? In that case, I would only be hiding You from myself, not myself from You.

But now, my sighs are sufficient evidence that I am displeased with myself; that You are my light and the source of my joy; that You are loved and desired. I am thoroughly ashamed of myself; I have renounced myself and chosen You, recognizing that I can please neither You nor myself unless You enable me to do so.

¶ 132 • _____ • **On Psalm 37** • If your desire lies open to God, who is your Father and sees in secret, He will answer you. For the desire of your heart is itself your prayer. . . . Therefore, if you wish to pray without ceasing, do not cease to desire. . . . It never ceases to sound in the hearing of God.

¶ 133 • _____ • **On Psalm 60** • Our pilgrimage on earth cannot be exempt from trial. We make progress by means of trial. No one knows himself except through trial, or receives a cross except after a victory, or strives except against an enemy or temptations.

¶ 134 • _____ • **On Psalm 85** • When we speak with God in prayer we do not separate the Son from Him, and when the body of the Son prays it does not separate its Head from itself; it is the one Savior of His Body, Our Lord Jesus Christ, the Son of God, who prays for us and in us and is himself the object of our prayers.

He prays for us as our Priest; He prays in us as our Head; He is the object of our prayers as our God.

¶ 135 • _____ • **On Psalm 109** • God, who is faithful, put Himself in our debt, not by receiving anything from us but by promising so much.

¶ 136 • _____ • **On the First Letter of John, No. 4** • The entire life of a good Christian is, in fact, an exercise of holy desire.

You do not yet see what you long for, but the very act of desiring prepares you, so that when He comes to you, you may see and be utterly satisfied.

¶ 137 • _____ • **On the Gospel of John, No. 5** • Heresies and other wicked teachings which ensnare souls and cast them into the deep, arise only when Holy Scripture is poorly understood, and what is not well understood in them is then affirmed with daring rashness.

¶ 138 • _____ • **On the Gospel of John, No. 124** • The Church recognizes two kinds of life as having been commanded to her by God. One is a life of faith, the other a life of vision; one is a life passed on pilgrimage in time, the other a dwelling place in eternity; one is a life of toil, the other of repose; one is spent on the road, the other in our homeland; one is active, involving labor, the other contemplative, the reward of the labor.

¶ 139 • **Celestine I, Pope St. †432** • **On St. Augustine** • We have ever had in communion with us Augustine of recent memory for the sake of his life and merits; never has the slightest breath of evil suspicion tarnished his name. We have always kept him in memory as a man of such great learning that my predecessors ranked him with the foremost masters. Unanimously they held him in high esteem, for all loved him and paid him honor.

¶ 140 • **Cassian, John, St. (c. 360 - c. 435)** • **Conference 10** • He prays too little who only prays when he is on his knees. But he never prays who, while on his knees, is in his heart roaming the fields.

¶ 141 • _____ • **On the Incarnation, 2:2** • And so you say, O heretic, whoever you may be, who deny that God was born of the Virgin, that Mary, the mother of Our Lord Jesus Christ ought not to be called *Theotokos* (Mother of God) but *Christotokos* (Mother of Christ, not of God). For no one, you say, brings forth what is anterior in time. . . . We will now go on to prove by divine witness that Christ is God and that Mary is therefore the Mother of God.

¶ 142 • **Cyril of Alexandria, St. †444 • Commentary on John, No. 10 •** After Christ had completed His mission on earth, it still remained necessary for us to become sharers in the divine nature of the Word. We had to give up our own life and be so transformed that we would begin to live an entirely new kind of life that would be pleasing to God. This was something we could do only by sharing in the Holy Spirit.

¶ 143 • _____ • **Letter 1 •** That anyone could doubt the right of the holy Virgin to be called the Mother of God fills me with astonishment. Surely she must be the Mother of God if Our Lord Jesus Christ is God and she gave birth to Him! Our Lord's disciples may not have used these exact words, but they delivered to us the belief those words enshrine, and this also has been taught to us by the holy Fathers.

¶ 144 • _____ • **First Letter to Nestorius •** This is the doctrine which strict orthodoxy everywhere prescribes. Thus shall we find the holy Fathers to have held. So they made bold to call the holy virgin *Theotokos* (God-bearer, i.e., Mother of God). Not as though the nature of the Word or His godhead had its beginning from the holy Virgin, but forasmuch as His holy Body, endued with a rational soul, was born of her, to which Body also the Word was personally (hypostatically) united, on this account He is said to have been born after the flesh.

¶ 145 • **Peter Chrysologus, St. †450 • Sermon 43 •** There are three things by which faith stands firm, devotion remains constant, and virtue endures. They are prayer, fasting, and mercy.

Prayer knocks at the door, fasting obtains, and mercy receives. . . .

Fasting is the soul of prayer; mercy is the lifeblood of fasting. Fasting bears no fruit unless it is watered by mercy. Fasting dries up when mercy dries up. Mercy is to fasting as rain is to the earth.

¶146 • _____ • **Sermon 147** • It is intolerable for love not to see the object of its longing. That is why whatever reward they merited was nothing to the saints if they could not see the Lord. A love that desires to see God may not have reasonableness on its side, but it is the evidence of filial love.

¶147 • **Leo I, the Great, Pope St. †461** • **Letter 28 to Flavius, No. 3** • Christ took the nature of a servant without stain of sin, enlarging our humanity without diminishing His divinity. He emptied himself; though invisible, He made himself visible; though Creator of all things, He chose to be one of us mortal men.

Yet this was the condescension of compassion, not the loss of omnipotence. So He, who in the nature of God had created man, became in the nature of a servant, man himself.

¶148 • _____ • **First Sermon on Christmas** • Christian, remember your dignity, and now that you share in God's own nature, do not return by sin to your former base condition. Bear in mind who is your Head and of whose Body you are a member.

Through the Sacrament of Baptism you have become a temple of the Holy Spirit.

¶149 • _____ • **Sixth Sermon on Christmas** • But what can we find in the treasure of the Lord's bounty but that peace which was first announced by the angelic choir on the day of His birth? That peace, from which the children of God spring, sustains love and mothers unity; it refreshes the blessed and shelters eternity; its characteristic function and special blessing are to join to God those whom it separates from the world.

¶ **150** • _____ • **Seventh Sermon on Christmas** • The man who rejoices in today's feast is a man of true devotion and reverence, with no false notions of the Incarnation of the Lord or of the Deity. It would be equally false to deny that Christ has a truly human nature like ours, as it would be to deny that He is equal in glory to the Father.

When we attempt to understand the mystery of the Nativity of Christ, who was born of a Virgin Mother, the mists of earthly reason must be banished and the smoke of mundane wisdom must be swept from eyes illuminated by faith.

We believe on divine authority. We follow a divine doctrine.

¶ **151** • _____ • **Sixth Sermon on Lent** • There is no more profitable practice as a companion to holy and spiritual fasting than that of almsgiving. This embraces under the single name of mercy many excellent works of devotion, so that the good intentions of all the faithful may be of equal value, even where their means are not.

Those who are unequal in their capacity to give can be equal in the love within their hearts.

¶ **152** • _____ • **Eighth Sermon on the Passion** • How marvelous the power of the cross, how great beyond all telling the glory of the passion — here is the judgment seat of the Lord, the condemnation of the world, the supremacy of Christ crucified.

The different sacrifices of animals are no more. The one offering of Your Body and Blood is the fulfillment of all the different sacrificial offerings, for You are the true Lamb of

God who takes away the sins of the world. In Yourself, You bring to perfection all mysteries.

¶153 • _____ • **Letter 31** • The divine nature and the nature of a servant were to be united in one person so that the Creator of time might be born in time, and that He through whom all things were made might be brought forth in their midst.

¶154 • **Elpis †493** • **Egregie Doctor Paule, v. 1** • Our soul's great teacher, Paul, / our guide in wisdom's way, / Teach us, our fainting hearts, / to heaven's glad clime to rise, / Till faith in clearest light / her bright meridian gains, / And love with sun-like fire / within each bosom reigns.

¶155 • **Gelasius I, Pope St. †496** • **Letter 12:3** • Nobody at any time or under whatever human pretext may proudly set himself above the office of him who by Christ's order was set above all and everyone, and whom the universal Church has always recognized as its head.

¶156 • **Vincent of Lérins, St. †c. 450** • **Commonitoria, 29** • It always was, and is today, the usual practice of Catholics to test the true Faith by two methods: first by the authority of the Divine Canon, and then by the Tradition of the Catholic Church.

Not that the Canon is unsufficient in itself in each case, but because most false interpretors of the Divine Word make use of their own arbitrary judgment and thus fall into various opinions and errors, the understanding of Holy Scripture must conform to the single rule of Catholic teaching — and this especially in regard to those questions upon which the foundations of all Catholic dogmas are laid.

¶157 • _____ • **First Instruction, No. 20** • He is the true and genuine Catholic who loves the truth of God, who loves the

Church, who loves the Body of Christ, who esteems divine religion and the Catholic Faith above everything else.

¶158 • _____ • **First Instruction, No. 23** • Is there to be no development of religion in the Church of Christ? Certainly there is to be development, and on the largest scale.

It must be true development of the Faith, not alteration. Development means that each thing expands to be itself, while alteration means that a thing is changed from one thing into another.

¶159 • **Sedulius Caelius †c. 450** • **A Solis Ortus Ordine, vv. 3, 4** • In that chaste parent's holy womb / Celestial grace has found its home; / And she, as earthly bride unknown, / Yet calls that Offspring blest her own.

The mansion of the modest breast / Becomes a shrine where God shall rest; / The pure and undefiled one / Conceived in her womb, the Son.

¶160 • _____ • **Crudelis Herodes, Deum, vv. 1, 2** • Why, impious Herod, vainly fear, / That Christ the Savior cometh here? / He takes no earthly realms away / Who gives the crown that lasts for aye.

To greet His birth the Wise Men went / Led by the star before them sent; / Called on by light, toward Light they pressed, / And by their gifts their God confessed.

[3]
The Times of Pope Gregory the Great

Although St. Bernard is called "The Last of the Fathers," the flourishing of the Patristic Age was over by the end of the fifth century.

The Roman Empire, first divided in two, was soon to be little more than an enclave in central Italy and a faltering giant on the Bosporus.

Petty kingdoms were springing up all over the continent of Europe. They were usually at war with one another, a pattern that was being set up for the next five centuries or so. The very names of many of these warring factions are now known only to historians dedicated to the study of this sorry period.

Some names do stand out. For a short time it looked as if the military policies of Belisarius might save some of the Roman power, but he had no capable successor.

Justinian was rightly famous for his work with the justice system, and he brought honor and dignity to the title of Emperor, but again, his successors were not up to his mettle, and his work survives as a monument of jurisprudence.

St. Benedict, the Father of Western Monasticism, lived in this turbulent era, and he has left an enduring monument to his name and work.

It was his genius that produced the "Holy Rule," that remarkable collection of regulations for monastic living. He was repelled by what he thought was the excessive austerity of the Eastern monks, and he made moderation the key to spiritual growth for his disciples.

In an age of growing instability, he introduced the rule of stability, which prohibited monks from one monastery from wandering off to some other establishment.

He combined the ethos of "work and prayer," *ora et labora,* so that his monasteries soon became well established and self-supported, enduring, as the centuries grew on, as beacons of light and hope that guaranteed that the best of the Roman civilization would be preserved and handed on.

Most of the Bible manuscripts that survive are copies that were carefully and lovingly copied by Benedictine monks. In the centuries before printing, their monastic scriptoria and libraries were almost the sole deposits of European learning.

Then, of course, came Pope Gregory I, "the Great." He was the last ray of hope before the darkness descended on Europe.

During his reign, the papacy began to accept the role thrust upon it by the lack of political and civil government in Italy. There was a power vacuum, and only the popes had the followers and the organization to accept the leadership role.

At the time it was a necessity. Whether it was good for the Church to become so involved in politics is a debatable question. I do not think it was good in the long run, but it's so easy to judge when one looks backward. The Church never really found a graceful way to back out of this role until the papacy was forced into abdication of political power, in 1870 by the unification of Italy, and in 1929 by the signing of the Vatican Concordat. There is no doubt in my mind that the Church is always stronger when it emphasizes its spiritual role.

Pope Gregory sent St. Augustine of Canterbury to England to begin the long history of Christianity in that realm. During the Pope's lifetime, St. Paul's Cathedral was begun in London, and St. Andrew's Cathedral in Rochester, England. It was also the time when St. Columban led a dozen monks to the continent from Ireland, a missionary project that still goes on.

In other parts of the world, the Sui Dynasty rose in China and the Toltec reign flourished in Mexico. Also, Muhammed was born in Mecca during this era.

¶161 • **Prosper of Aquitaine, St. †c. 456 • Call of All Nations, 1:24 •**
The evidence from Scripture demonstrates abundantly, I
think, that the faith which justifies a sinner cannot be had
except for God's gift, and that it is not a reward for previous
merits. Rather it is given that it may be a source of merit, and
while it is itself given unprayed for, the prayers it inspires
obtain all other favors.

¶162 • **Patrick, St. (389 - 461) • Canons (attributed to him), No. 6 •** If
any cleric, from sexton to priest, is seen without his tunic,
and does not cover the same and the nakedness of his body,
and if his hair is not shaven according to the Roman custom,
and if his wife goes about with her head unveiled, he shall be
despised alike by laymen and separated from the Church.

¶163 • **Theodoret of Cyr †c. 466 • Letter 89 •** I have ever kept
the faith of the Apostles undefiled. I have learned not only
from the Apostles and the prophets, but also from those who
interpreted their teachings: Ignatius, Athanasius, Basil,
Gregory, John, and the rest of the lights of the world. I also
preserve, in its integrity, the profession of faith from the holy
Fathers in Council at Nicea.

¶164 • **Pomerius, Julianus †c. 500 • On the Contemplative Life, 2:22**
• In the active life, a man makes progress though beset with
the difficulties incident to our human life. He controls the
rebellions of his bodily nature, curbing them by his reason.
    But the aim of the contemplative is to mount, through his
desire of perfection, above merely human things; the active
life means progress; the contemplative has reached the goal;
the former makes a man holy; the latter makes him perfect.

¶165 • **Boethius †c. 524 • The Consolation of Philosophy, 3: poem 9 •**
Grant, O Father, that my mind may rise to Your sacred
throne. Let it see the fountain of good; let it find light, so that
the clear light of my soul may fix itself in You.

Burn off the fogs and clouds of earth and shine through in
Your splendor. For You are the serenity, the tranquil peace of
virtuous men. The sight of You is the beginning and the end;
one guide, leader, path, and goal.

¶166 • _____ • **The Consolation of Philosophy, 3: prose 10** • We
must agree that the most high God is full of the highest and
most perfect good. But we have already established that
perfect good is true happiness; therefore, it follows that true
happiness has its dwelling in the most high God.

¶167 • **Caesarius of Arles, St. †c. 502** • **Sermon 25** • What sort of
people are we? When God gives, we wish to receive, but
when He begs, we refuse to give. Remember, it was Christ
who said, "I was hungry and you did not feed me." When the
poor are starving, Christ also hungers.

Do not neglect to improve the unhappy condition of the
poor if you wish to be sure that your own sins are forgiven.
Christ hungers now, my brethren; it is He who deigns to
hunger and thirst in the persons of the poor. What He will
return in heaven tomorrow is what He receives here on earth
today.

¶168 • **Benedict of Nursia, St. (c. 480 - 547)** • **Holy Rule, Prologue** •
Girded with faith and the performance of good works, let us
follow the path of Christ by the guidance of the Holy Gospel.
Then we shall deserve to see Him who has called us into His
own kingdom. If we wish to attain a dwelling-place in His
kingdom, we shall not reach it unless we hasten there by our
good deeds.

¶169 • _____ • **"Tools of Good Works," Rule: 4 passim** • To
utter truth from the heart and mouth. / To reverence the old,
to love the young. / To hate one's own self-will. / When evil
thoughts come into one's heart, to dash them at once on the
Rock of Christ and to manifest them to one's spiritual

father. / To keep one's mouth from evil and depraved talk; not to love much speaking. / To fulfill God's commandments daily in one's deed. / To listen gladly to spiritual reading.

¶170 • Fulgentius of Ruspe, St. (6th cent.) • Third Sermon • Love is the source of all good things. It is an impregnable defense and the way that leads to heaven. He who walks in love can neither go astray nor be afraid. Love guides him, protects him, and brings him to his journey's end.

Christ made love the stairway to heaven.

¶171 • _____ • To Monimus, No. 2 • The Holy Trinity, the one true God, is of its nature unity, equality, and love, and by one divine activity sanctifies its adopted sons.

¶172 • _____ • Treatise on Faith, No. 3 • From the time when the Savior said to us, "If anyone is not born again from water and the Holy Spirit, he cannot enter into the kingdom of Heaven" (Jn. 3:15), without the sacrament of Baptism — apart from those who, without Baptism in the Catholic Church, shed their blood for Christ — no one can receive the Kingdom of God or eternal life.

¶173 • _____ • Treatise in the Faith, No. 22 • Christ is the priest through whom we have been reconciled, the sacrifice by which we have been reconciled, the temple in which we have been reconciled, the God with whom we have been reconciled.

Now in the time of the New Testament the holy Catholic Church throughout the world never ceases to offer the sacrifice of bread and wine, in faith and love, to Him and to the Father and the Holy Spirit, with whom He shares one godhead.

¶174 • Gregory, the Great, Pope St. (c. 540 - 604) • Dialogues 4:48 • This Sacrifice [the Mass] alone has the power of saving the soul from eternal death, for it presents to us, mystically, the death of the only-begotten Son. Though He is now risen from the dead and can die no more, and "death has no more power over Him" (Rom. 6:9), yet, living in himself immortal and incorruptible, He is again immolated for us in the mystery of the Holy Sacrifice.

Where His Body is eaten, there His Flesh is distributed among the people for their salvation. His Blood no longer stains the godless hands, but flows into the hearts of His faithful followers. See, then, how august the Sacrifice that is offered for us, ever reproducing in itself the passion of the only-begotten Son for the remission of our sins.

¶175 • _____ • **Ex More Docti Mystico, vv. 1, 2** • The fast, as taught by holy lore, / We keep in solemn course once more: / The fast to all men known and bound / In forty days of yearly round.

The laws and seers that were of old / In differing ways this Lent foretold, / Which Christ, all seasons' King and Guide, / In after ages sanctified.

¶176 • _____ • **Homily 26** • The disbelief of Thomas has done more for our faith than the faith of all the other disciples. . . .

As he touches Christ and is won over to belief, every doubt is cast away and our faith is strengthened. The disciple who doubted, but then felt Christ's wounds, becomes a witness to the reality of Christ's Resurrection. Touching Christ, he cried out, "My Lord and My God!"

¶177 • _____ • **Homily 26** • What follows is reason for great joy: "Blessed are those who have not seen and have believed." There is here a particular reference to ourselves. We hold in our hearts One we have not seen in the flesh.

We are included in these words, but only if we follow up our faith with good works. The true believer practices what

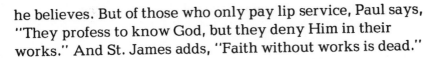

he believes. But of those who only pay lip service, Paul says,
"They profess to know God, but they deny Him in their
works." And St. James adds, "Faith without works is dead."

¶178 • _____ • **Homily 34** • Personal names are applied to
some [archangels] to denote their ministry when they come
among us. Thus, Michael means "Who is like God?" and
Raphael is "God's Remedy"; and Gabriel is "The Strength of
God."

¶179 • _____ • **Hominis Superne Conditor, vv. 1, 2** • Maker of
man, who from Your throne / Ordered all things, God
alone; / By whose decree the teeming earth / To reptile and
to beast gave birth.
　　The mighty forms that fill the land, / Instinct with life at
your command, / Are given subdued to humankind / For
service in their rank assigned.

¶180 • _____ • **Moral Reflections on Job, Bk. 10** • It is the
wisdom of this world to conceal the heart with strategems, to
veil one's thoughts with words, to make what is false appear
true and what is true appear false. On the other hand, it is the
wisdom of the just never to pretend anything for show,
always to use words to express one's thoughts, to love the
truth as it is and to avoid what is false, to do what is right
without reward and to be more willing to put up with evil
than to perpetrate it, not to seek revenge for wrong, and to
consider as gain any insult for truth's sake.

¶181 • _____ • **Primo Die, Quo Trinitas** • Hail day! in which
the Trinity / First formed the earth by sure decree; / The day
its Maker rose again, / And vanquished death and burst our
chain.
　　Away with sleep and slothful ease! / We raise our hearts

and bend our knees / And early seek the Lord of
all, / Obedient to the prophet's call.

¶182 • **Fortunatus, Venantius (530 - 609)** • **Pange Lingua Gloriosi,
vv. 1, 6** • Sing, my tongue, the glorious battle, / Sing the last,
the dread affray; / O'er the cross the victor's trophy, / Sing
the high triumphal lay: / Tell how Christ, the world's
Redeemer, / As a Victim won the day.

Thirty years among us dwelling, / His appointed time
fulfilled, / Born for this, He meets His passion / For that this
He freely willed: / On the cross the Lamb is lifted / Where
His life-blood shall be spilled.

¶183 • _____ • **Quem Terra, Pontus, Sidera, vv. 1, 3** • The God
whom earth and sea and sky / Adore and laud and
magnify, / Who o'er their threefold fabric reigns, / The
Virgin's spotless womb contains.

How blest that Mother in whose shrine / The great
Artificer Divine, / Whose hand contains the earth and
sky, / Vouchsafed, as in His Ark, to lie.

¶184 • _____ • **Vexilla Regis Prodeunt, vv. 1, 3** • Abroad the
regal banners fly, / Now shines the cross's mystery; / Upon
it Life did death endure, / And yet by death did life procure.

That which the prophet-king of old / Had in mysterious
verse foretold, / Is now accomplished, while we see / God
ruling nations from a tree.

¶185 • **Isidore of Seville, St. (566 - 636)** • **Book of Maxims, No. 3** • If
a man wants to be continually in God's presence, he must
pray regularly and read regularly. When we pray, we talk to
God. When we read, God talks to us.

All spiritual growth comes from reading and reflection.
By reading we learn what we did not know. By reflection we
retain what we have learned.

¶186 • _____ • **On the Supreme Good, 3:15** • In the active life the vices are to be removed first by the practice of good works, so that in the contemplative life a man may, now with purified mental gaze, pass to the contemplation of the divine Light.

[4]

Darkness Falls Over Europe

This next period is usually referred to as "The Dark Ages," but the name is not quite exact. There was not the flurry of intellectual activity witnessed in previous ages, and culture never approached anywhere near the ferment of the Renaissance, but it was not a sterile time.

The pace was slower during these five centuries as Europe groped its way toward a different political organization. The Holy Roman Empire was never more than a shadow of the might of the empire it finally replaced, and as someone has remarked, it was neither holy nor, for that matter, Roman.

It was the age of valiant missionary work, when nation after nation, as we know them today, gradually became Catholic and established bishoprics. The Irish missionaries roamed far and wide, planting the Faith firmly. No doubt they reached North America to the West and Russia to the East.

With Latin the common tongue, scholars went back and forth between various capitals, universities, and monasteries. There was a much broader exchange of cultural and intellectual activity than is generally realized, possibly because the pace was much slower and there were fewer examples of outstanding minds.

During this time the Cluny branch of the Benedictines was formed, and it exercised much influence for two centuries. Near the end of this period the Cistercians were also founded — an order which started as a "reformed" Benedictine branch but very quickly became a separate Order with tremendous influence.

Probably the most interesting scientific event of this entire period was the introduction, from India through the Arabs, of the zero in arithmetic. This made the decimal system with its multiplication and division by tens a real, practical advance. There were also some medical advances, mostly through the Arabs.

However, the Muslim Arabians became the scourge of the Christian world. Their hatred for Christians and Jews was almost implacable. The ancient Churches of Palestine, Turkey, Egypt, and North Africa fell before their swords. They made inroads into Spain and eastern Europe before united Christian effort could become effective. This would later lead to several Crusades which, though noble in their intent to free the Christian Holy Lands, lost their nobility quickly in practice.

The same judgment has to be made about the Inquisition in the next age — noble in its attempt to prevent the cancer of heresy, but so quickly abused when put into practice. Again, we must be careful not to judge by our standards, or by hindsight.

In Rome the papacy went through its darkest hours in the tenth century, when certain Italian families "captured" it and made it a part of their own use of power. If the Church of Christ were only a human institution, it would surely have died then!

But the Spirit of God is with the Catholic Church, to bring it through dark ages when all seems lost, and through triumphant times when all seems glorious. Who knows which are the more trying times?

In other parts of the world, probably the two most interesting items, for us, were the founding of Machu Picchu in Peru and the rise of the Pueblo cultures in what is now the southwestern part of the United States. In the fields of art, music, and architecture, there was a steady growth in the movements that would explode on the scene in the next age, but of masterpieces there were precious few.

One bright aspect, if unsuccessful, was the effort the
Church made to provide the use of "sanctuary." We shall see
a couple of examples of this attempt in the next few pages.

¶187 • **Columban, St. †615** • **Christ, the Fountain of Life, No. 2** • If
you thirst, drink of the fountain of life; if you are hungry, eat
the bread of life. Blessed are they who hunger for this bread
and thirst for this fountain, for in so doing they will desire
ever more to eat and to drink.

For what they eat and drink is especially sweet, and their
thirst and appetite for more is never satisfied. Though it is
ever tasted, it is ever more desired. Thus King David says,
"Taste and see how sweet is the Lord!"

¶188 • **Modestus of Jerusalem, St. †c. 634** • **On the Assumption, No.
14** • As the most glorious Mother of Christ, our Savior and
God and the Giver of life and immortality, has been endowed
with life by Him, she has received an eternal incorruptibility
of the body together with Him who has raised her up from the
tomb and has taken her up to himself in a way known only to
Him.

¶189 • **Sophronius, St. †638** • **On the Annunciation** • Truly you,
O Mary, are blessed among all women, because while
remaining a woman, a creature of our race, you have become
the Mother of God. For if the Holy One born of your womb is
truly God Incarnate, then must you truly be called the
Mother of God, since you have, in absolute truth, brought
forth God.

¶190 • _____ • **Sermon 3** • By faith we have embraced
Christ, the salvation of God the Father, as He came to us from
Bethlehem. Gentiles before, we have now become the People
of God. Our eyes have seen God Incarnate, and because we
have seen Him present among us and have mentally received

Him into our arms, we are called the New Israel. Never shall we forget His presence.

¶191 • **Roman Breviary (7th cent.)** • **O Antiphons 2, 7** • O Adonai and Leader of the House of Israel, who appeared to Moses in the burning bush and gave him the law on Mt. Sinai: come and redeem us with Your outstretched arm. . . .

O Emmanuel, our King and Lawgiver, the expectation of all the nations and their Savior: come and save us, O Lord our God.

¶192 • **Maximus the Confessor, St. †662** • **Centuries on Charity 1:98** • We do not know God in His essence but by the grandeur of His creation and the action of His Providence, which present to us, as in a mirror, the reflection of His infinite goodness, wisdom, and power.

¶193 • **Ine, King of Wessex †c. 680** • **Legal Decrees** • 5. If anyone is liable to the death penalty, and he flees to a Church, his life shall be spared and he shall pay such compensation as he is directed to by legal decision.

5:1. If anyone renders himself liable to the lash and flees to the Church, he shall be immune from scourging.

¶194 • **Andrew of Crete, St. (660 - 740)** • **Great Canon, Lent** • O supersubstantial Trinity that art adored in Unity, remove from me the heavy yoke of my sins, and in Thy great mercy grant me tears of repentance. . . .

Whence shall I begin to bewail the deeds of my miserable life? What beginning shall I make, O Christ, of my present complaint? Do Thou, O merciful One, grant me the forgiveness of my trespasses.

¶195 • **Bede the Venerable, St. (673 - 735)** • **Commentary on I Peter, No. 2** • The deliverance of the children of Israel and their

journey to the long-promised land correspond with the
mystery of our redemption. We are making our way toward
the light of our heavenly home with the grace of Christ
leading us and showing us the way.

¶ 196 • _____ • **Homily** • It is an excellent and fruitful
custom of Holy Church that we should sing Mary's hymn
[the Magnificat] at the time of evening prayer. By meditating
on the Incarnation, our devotion is kindled, and by
remembering the example of God's mother, we are
encouraged to lead a life of virtue.

¶ 197 • **John Damascene, St. (c. 675 - 749)** • **The Statement of Faith** •
And you, O Church, are a most excellent assembly, the noble
summit of perfect integrity, whose assistance comes from
God. You, devout Christians, receive from us a statement of
the Faith that is free from error, to strengthen the Church,
just as our fathers handed it down to us.

¶ 198 • _____ • **The Statement of Faith** • Moreover, we
proclaim the holy Virgin to be in strict truth the Mother of
God. For inasmuch as He who was born of her was true God,
she who bore Him, the true Incarnate God, is the true Mother
of God. For we hold that God was born of her, not implying
that the divinity of the Word received from her the beginning
of its being, but meaning that God the Word himself, who
was begotten of the Father timelessly before the ages, and
was with the Father and the Spirit without beginning and
through eternity, took up His abode in these last days for the
sake of our salvation in the Virgin's womb, and was without
change made flesh and born of her.

¶ 199 • **Paulinus, St. (750 - 802)** • **Quodcumque in Orbe, v. 1** •
Peter, whatever you shall bind on earth, / The same is bound
above the starry sky; / What here your delegated power shall

loose, / Is loosed in heaven's court on high. / To judgment you shall come when the world's end is nigh.

¶200 • **Alcuin of York (735 - 804)** • **Commentary on the Epistle to Titus, Ch. 1** • Above everything, hospitality is prescribed for one who is to be a bishop, for if everyone wants to hear from the Gospel, "I was a stranger and you took me in," how much more should a bishop, whose house ought to be a common guesthouse and in it those pilgrims who came should be kindly received?

A bishop ought to be just and holy, and to practice justice among the people over whom he is placed, and not to show any respect of persons in his judgment but decide justly for every person; and holy with respect to his life, so as not only to teach with words, but also to instruct the people entrusted to him by his example.

¶201 • **Mayence (Mainz), Council of (813)** • **Decrees** • Let no one dare to remove a wrongdoer who has fled to a church, nor give him up from there for punishment or death, that the honor of the churches may be preserved; but let the rectors be diligent in securing his life and limb. Nevertheless, he must lawfully compound for whatever he has done wrongfully.

¶202 • **Theodulf of Orléans †821** • **Gloria, Laus, et Honor, vv. 1, 3** • All glory, laud, and honor, / To Thee, Redeemer King, / To whom the lips of children / Made sweet Hosannas ring.

Thou art the King of Israel, / Thou, David's royal Son, / Who in the Lord's name cometh, / The King and Blessed One.

¶203 • **Smaragdus, Abbot †c. 830** • **The Royal Way, 8, 9** • Therefore, O king, love justice and judgment, the royal road, which has been trodden by former kings from of old. . . . But temper justice and diligently guard against left-handed cruelty. . . .

If you wish your throne to be firmly established by the Lord, O king, do not cease to do justice to the poor and the orphaned.

¶204 • Jonas of Orléans †843 On the Institution of Kings • It is the king's chief duty to govern the people of God and rule them with equity and justice, and to work for them to have peace and concord. First of all, he must be a defender of the churches and the servants of God. . . . The needs of widows, orphans, the poor, and indeed all the needy should be attended.

¶205 • Rabanus Maurus, Bl. (c. 776 - 856) • Veni Creator Spiritus, vv. 1, 2 • Creator Spirit all-divine, / Come and visit every soul / And fill with Your celestial flame / The hearts which You Yourself have framed.

O Gift of God, Yours is the sweet / Consoling name of Paraclete — / And spring of life and fire and love / And unction flowing from above.

¶206 • Paschasius Radbertus, St. (c. 785 - c. 860) • The Lord's Body and Blood, No. 1 • Of the sacrament of the Lord's Body and Blood daily celebrated in the Church, no one of the faithful ought to be ignorant or unaware of what in it pertains to faith and what to knowledge, because faith in the mystery is not rightly defended without knowledge, nor is knowledge nurtured without faith.

¶207 • Scotus, John Erigena †c. 877 • On the Division of Nature, 1:50, 68 • When I say, "I understand that I am," do I not signify by this one word "understand" three inseparable things? For I prove that I am, that I can understand that I am, and that I do understand that I am. . . .

No vice is found but in the shadow of some virtue.

¶208 • **Methodius, St. †885** • **On Free Will, Ch. 12** • I began to praise the Creator as I saw the earth firmly stable, and living creatures in such a variety, and the blossoms of plants with their many hues. It is the nature of things which come into existence to derive their origin from what is already existing. And it seemed to me that it might be said with equal truth that nothing is eternally co-existent with God distinct from himself, but that whatever exists has its origin from Him, and I was persuaded of this also by the undeniable disposition of the elements, and by the orderly arrangement of nature about them.

¶209 • **Alfred the Great, King †899** • **Grant of Asylum** • 2. If a man flees for any manner of offense to a monastery which is entitled to receive the king's food-rent, or to any other free community which is endowed, for the space of three days he shall have asylum, unless he is willing to come to terms.

¶210 • **Odo of Cluny, St. (879 - 942)** • **Summi Parentis Unice, vv. 1, 3** • Son of the Highest, deign to cast / On us a pitying eye, / You who repentent Magdalen / Called to endless joy.
O Jesus, balm of every wound! / The sinner's only stay! / Wash in Magdalene's pure tears / Our guilty spots away.

¶211 • **Vladimir, St. †1015** • **Envoy's Report*** • The Greeks led us to the edifices where they worship their God and we knew not whether we were in heaven or on earth. For on earth there is no splendor or beauty such as this, and we are at a loss how to describe it. We only know that God dwells there among men and their service is fairer than the ceremonies of other nations. For we cannot forget that beauty. [*Some historians question the authenticity of this report.]

¶212 • **Wipo †c. 1047** • **Victimae Paschali, v. 1** • Christ the Lord is risen today; / Christians, haste your vows to pay, / Offer

you your praises meet / At the Paschal Victim's feet; / For
the sheep the Lamb has bled, / Sinless in the sinner's
stead. / Christ the Lord is risen on high; / Now He lives, no
more to die.

¶213 • **Hermannus Contractus (1013 - 1054)** • **Alma Redemptoris
Mater, vv. 1, 2** • Mother benign of our redeeming Lord, / Star of
the Sea and portal of the skies, / Unto your fallen people help
afford — / Fallen, but striving still anew to rise.

You who once while wondering worlds adored, / Bore
your Creator, Virgin then as now, / O by your holy joy at
Gabriel's word, / Pity the sinners who now before you bow.

¶214 • _____ • **Salve Regina (prose version)** • Hail Holy
Queen, mother of mercy, our life, our sweetness and our
hope. To you do we cry, poor banished children of Eve. To
you do we send up our sighs, mourning and weeping in this
vale of tears. Turn then, most gracious advocate, your eyes of
mercy toward us, and after this, our exile, show us the fruit
of your womb, Jesus.

*O clement, O loving, O sweet Virgin Mary! [*This is
considered an addition made much later by St. Bernard.]

¶215 • **Peter Damian, St. (1007 - 1072)** • **Dominus Vobiscum, Ch. 8** •
So great is the unity of the Church in Christ that throughout
the whole world there is but one Bread which is the Body of
Christ and one chalice which is the Chalice of His Blood. Just
as the divinity of the Word of God is one and fills the whole
world, so although that Body is consecrated in many places
and on many days, yet there are not many bodies but the one
Body of Christ.

And just as this Bread and Wine are truly changed into
the Body of Christ, so all those who partake of it worthily in
the Church are made into the one Body of Christ, as He
himself bore witness when He said, "He that eats my flesh
and drinks my blood lives in me and I in him."

¶216 • **Gregory VII (Hildebrand), Pope St. †1085** • **Dictatus Papae** • The Roman Church has never erred, and according to the Scriptures, it never shall err.

He cannot be accounted a Catholic who does not agree with the Roman Church.

The Roman Pontiff alone can be called universal.

¶217 • **Berengarius of Tours (1000 - 1088)** • **Statement** • I firmly believe . . . that the bread and wine which are laid on the altar, by the mystery of sacred prayer and the words of our Redeemer, are substantially converted into the very flesh and blood of Christ, true and life-giving; and that after the consecration it is the true Body of Christ which was born of the Virgin, which was offered as a sacrifice on the cross for the salvation of the world, and which sits at the right hand of the Father; and the very Blood of Christ which flowed from His side; and that the sacrament is to be understood not merely as a sign and virtually, but actually and really.

¶218 • **Anselm, St. †1109** • **Proslogion, Ch. 14** • My soul, have you found what you are looking for? You were looking for God and you have discovered that He is the Supreme Being, and that you could not possibly imagine anything more perfect. You have discovered that this Supreme Being is life itself, light, wisdom, goodness, eternal beatitude, and blessed eternity. He is everywhere and He is timeless. . . .

O God, let me know You and love You so that I may find my joy in You; and if I cannot do so fully in this life, let me at least make some progress daily, until at last that knowledge, love, and joy come to me in all their plenitude in heaven.

¶219 • _____ • **"Why the God-Man," 1:18** • When we say that God is subjected to some abasement or weakness, we do not understand this with regard to the sublimity of His impassible nature, but with regard to the weakness of the human substance He bore. We are not attributing any

abasement to the divine substance, but we are showing that
the God-Man is one person.

In the Incarnation of God there is no thought of any
abasement of God, but we do believe in the exaltation of the
nature of man.

¶220 • **Stephen Harding, St. †c. 1134 • Letter to the Cistercians** • We
enjoin upon you that you never presume through levity to
change or detract from the integrity of the Holy Rule [of St.
Benedict] which you know has been worked out and
established by us in this place with no little labor, but rather,
living as lovers, imitators, and defenders of our holy Father.

¶221 • **Hugh of Fleury †c. 1120 • Treatise on Royal Power, 1:2** •
The chief powers by which the world is ruled are two, the
royal and the priestly. Both powers Our Lord Jesus Christ
willed to bear himself in His person alone in a holy and
mysterious way, for He is both King and Priest: King because
He governs us; Priest because He has cleansed us by the
immolation of His own Body from the sordidness of our sins
and reconciled us to His Father.

¶222 • **Eadmer of Canterbury †1130 • On the Conception of St. Mary**
• All men sinned in Adam (Rom. 5:12). This statement is
certainly true and I declare it would be impious to deny it.
But when I consider the eminence of God's grace in you
[Mary], I find that in a truly remarkable way you were placed
not among but above all other creatures; hence I conclude
that in your conception you were not bound by the law of
nature like others, but by the extraordinary power and
operation of divinity, in a way transcending human reason,
you were preserved from all taint of sin.

¶223 • **Edward the Confessor, King †1066 • Laws** • If, however, a
man commits a crime repeatedly, and happens to take refuge

repeatedly in this way, after restoring what he has stolen he shall abjure the kingdom [in exile] and shall not return.

¶224 • **Rupert of Deutz †1130** • **The Victory of God's Word, No. 15** • Who does not know that all we who believe receive, or have received, through the death of Christ and His Blood, the gift of the Holy Spirit, first for the remission of sins? For that reason, on the day when He arose from the dead, late on that same day, He, standing in the midst of His disciples, "breathed on them and said, 'Receive the Holy Spirit.' " Then He added immediately, "Whose sins you remit they are remitted to them."

Later, on the fifteenth day, they received the second gift of the Holy Spirit for the distribution of graces, which the Apostle recalled when he wrote to the Corinthians, "To one is given through the Spirit the utterance of wisdom, to another the utterance of knowledge," etc.

¶225 • **Thurstan of York †1140** • **Letter of 1132** • These monks sought nothing but that they might follow the poor Christ in voluntary poverty, that they might carry the cross of Christ in their own bodies, that they might not be impeded from living in evangelical peace and observing the Rule of the blessed Father Benedict.

¶226 • **Hildebert of Lavardin †1133** • **Prayer to the Holy Trinity** • First and last of faith's receiving, / Source and Sea of man's believing, / God, whose might is all potential, / God, whose truth is truth's essential, / Good Supreme in Your subsisting, / Good is all You, seen existing / Over all things, all things under, / Touching all, from all asunder, / Center — You, but not intruded, / Compassing and yet included.

[5]
The Greatest of Centuries

Among the books that I treasure most in my own library is an autographed edition of James. J. Walsh's book *The Thirteenth, the Greatest of Centuries*. His thesis is that the people of that century did "more for human progress than those of any like period in human history."

Since the book has 458 pages, the author has assembled what he considers abundant proof of his theory. There was probably more intellectual ferment in that one century than in all of the preceding six or seven combined.

However, he does not make the case that it was an isolated time. In the two centuries before it, the ground swell of progress is clearly noted so that the Middle Ages reach their peak in the 1200s. After that it is all downhill, with the seeds of the Reformation clearly growing.

Walsh is impressed by the formation of the universities that were organized in most of the larger urban centers all over western and southern Europe. The academic freedom that they achieved was used profusely for the advancement of Christian knowledge. They had graduate faculties in all the major areas of the liberal arts, theology, philosophy, law, medicine, and science, as they understood them.

The great Gothic cathedrals are also monuments to the genius of the thirteenth century. They dotted France, Spain, England, the Germanys, and Italy. They are the enduring stone books of medieval art. Think of the magnificent stained glass of Lincoln, York, Chartres, and Bourges, to mention only a few.

To try to chronicle the artists, sculptors, and musicians of this period would tax the scope of this volume. Medieval poets and romances flourished; their libraries were of a growing and inquiring kind, and they had the literature to go along with it — The Cid, King Arthur and the Holy Grail, the Nibelungen, the Song of Roland, and the Romance of the Rose.

The mystery plays are probably the ancestors of modern drama. The great Latin hymns were the envy of later centuries.

And the names! St. Francis of Assisi, St. Thomas Aquinas, Louis IX, Dante, St. Dominic, St. Elizabeth of Hungary, Blanche of Castille, and Isabella of Aragon. And these are just a portion of the great lights of the thirteenth century.

Political development also showed progress, from the Magna Carta of England to the democracy of the German city-states. And it was an age that suddenly discovered there was more to the civilized world than just Europe.

The excerpts we bring together here will help us share the excitement of so great an age. That it had its darker side we must also acknowledge, with Crusades that failed, plagues, and infighting between warring neighbors. The papacy regained much of its luster and prestige, although the human imperfections remained.

In the wider context, Ghengis Khan consolidated his power and greatly increased his empire. Saladin was a Muslim power, and, in China, explosives were first used in warfare. Moses Maimonides was the great medieval Jewish philosopher, and Roger Bacon probably the first of the modern scientists.

Catholic "wisdom" took some giant steps forward in the thirteenth century and its neighboring times.

¶ 227 • **Abélard, Peter (1079 - 1142)** • **Know Yourself (Ethics): On Confession** • Finally, priests, to whom have been committed the souls of those who confess, have to impose satisfactions of

penance upon them, so that those who have used their
judgment wrongly and proudly, by showing contempt of
God, may be corrected by the judgment of another power.

¶228 • **Aelred, St. (1110 - 1167)** • **Mirror of Love, No. 3** •
Friendship is the most dangerous of all of our affections. . . .

It is such a great joy to have the consolation of someone's
affection — someone to whom we are deeply united by the
bonds of love, someone in whom our weary spirit may find
rest, and to whom we may pour out our souls, someone
whose conversation is as sweet as a song in the tedium of our
daily life.

¶229 • _____ • **On the Feast of St. Benedict, No. 3** • Indeed,
almighty God can bring to perfection immediately anyone He
pleases, and give each one all the virtues. But His loving
provision for us is such that each one needs the other, and
what anyone does not find in himself, he has in the other.
Thus, humility is preserved, love increased, and unity
realized.

¶230 • **Adam of St. Victor †c. 1150** • **Missus Gabriel** • Gabriel,
from heaven descending, / On the faithful Word
attending, / Is in holy converse blending / With the Virgin
full of grace.

That good world and sweet he plights, / In the bosom
where it lights, / And for EVA, AVE writes, / Changing Eva's
name and race.

¶231 • **Bernard of Morlas (Cluny) (12th cent.)** • **De Contemptu Mundi,**
vv. 1-3 • The world is very evil, / The times are waxing
late. / Be sober and keep vigil, / The Judge is at the gate.

The Judge that comes in mercy, / The Judge that comes
with might, / To terminate the evil, / To diadem the right.

Arise, arise, good Christian, / Let right to wrong
succeed. / Let penitential sorrow / To heavenly gladness
lead.

¶232 • **Guerric of Igny, Blessed †1157** • **Sermon 47, No. 3** • If the servant of Christ by his care and heartfelt tenderness bears his little children again and again until Christ is formed in them, how much more is this true of the very Mother of Christ? Paul begot his children by preaching the word of truth, through which they were born again; but Mary, in a manner far more holy and marvelous, by giving birth to the Word himself. I do indeed praise the ministry of preaching in Paul, but far more do I admire and venerate that mystery of generation in Mary.

¶233 • **Isaac of Stella †c. 1169** • **Sermon 31** • Charity is the reason why anything should be done or left undone, changed or left unchanged. It is the initial principle and the end to which all things should be directed. Whatever is honestly done out of love and in accordance with love can never be blameworthy.

The more any way of life sincerely strives for the love of God and the love of neighbor for God's sake, the more acceptable it is to God, no matter what its observance or external form.

¶234 • _____ • **Sermon 51** • The Son of God is the firstborn of many brothers. Although by nature He is the only-begotten, by grace He has joined many to himself and made them one with Him. For to those who receive Him, "He has given the power to become sons of God."

¶235 • _____ • **Sermon 11** • The Church is incapable of forgiving any sin without Christ, and Christ is unwilling to forgive any sin without the Church. The Church cannot forgive the sin of someone who has not repented, who has not been touched by Christ; Christ will not forgive the sin of one who despises the Church.

¶236 • **William of St. Thierry, Abbot †c. 1148** • **On the Contemplation of God** • You know that love cannot be forced on men's hearts,

my God, since You created love; it must rather be elicited.
And this for the further reason that there is no freedom
where there is compulsion, and where freedom is lacking —
so too, is righteousness.

¶237 • **Bernard of Cluny, St. (fl. 1150)** • **Omni Die Dic Mariae, v. 1** •
Daily, daily sing to Mary, / Sing, my soul, her praises
due: / All her feasts, her actions worship, / With the heart's
devotion true. / Lost in wondering contemplation / Be her
majesty confessed. / Call her Mother, call her
Virgin, / Happy Mother, Virgin blest.

¶238 • **Bernard of Clairvaux, St. (1090 - 1153)** • **Jesu Dulcis Memoria
vv. 3, 4** • O Hope of every contrite heart, / O Joy of all the
meek, / To those who fall, how kind You are, / How good to
those who seek!
But what to those who find? Ah! This / Nor tongue nor
pen can show: / The love of Jesus, what it is / None but His
loved ones know.

¶239 • _____ • **Misc. Sermons, No. 5** • The whole of the
spiritual life consists of these two elements. When we think
of ourselves, we are perturbed and filled with a salutary
sadness. When we think of the Lord, we are revived to find
consolation in the joy of the Holy Spirit. From the first we
derive fear and humility, and from the second hope and love.

¶240 • _____ • **Misc. Sermons, No. 15** • There are three
ways for wisdom, or prudence, to abound in you: if you
confess your sins, if you give thanks and praise, and if your
speech is edifying.

¶241 • _____ • **Missus Est, No. 1** • God submitting in
obedience to a woman is indeed humility without equal; the
woman commanding her God is sublime beyond measure. In
praising virgins, we read that they follow the Lamb wherever

He goes. How can we possibly praise enough the Virgin who leads Him?

Learn, O man, to obey. Learn, O earth, to be subject. Learn, O dust, to bow down. In speaking of our Creator, the evangelist says, "and He was subject to them," that is, to Mary and to Joseph.

¶242 • _____ • **Missus Est, No. 2** • When you find yourself tossed by the raging storms on this great sea of life, far from land, keep your eyes fixed on this star to avoid disaster. When the winds of temptation or the rocks of tribulation threaten, look up to the star, call upon Mary!

When the waves of pride or ambition sweep over you, when the tide of detraction or jealousy runs against you, look up to the star, call upon Mary! When the shipwreck of avarice, anger, or lust seems imminent, call upon Mary!

If the horror of sin overwhelms you and the voice of conscience terrifies you, if the fear of judgment, the abyss of sadness, and the depths of despair clutch at your heart, think of Mary! In danger, difficulties, and sins, think about Mary, call upon Mary!

¶243 • _____ • **On Advent, No. 5** • Keep God's word in this way: let it enter your very being, let it take possession of your desires and your whole way of life. Feed on goodness and your very soul will delight in its richness.

¶244 • _____ • **On the Canticle of Canticles, No. 15** • If someone writes a book, I cannot savor it unless it speaks to me of Jesus. If anyone speaks or preaches, I cannot enjoy it unless I find Jesus in it.

The name of Jesus is honey in the mouth, music to the ear, a cry of gladness in the heart!

¶245 • _____ • **On the Circumcision, No. 1** • The circumcision proves, beyond a shadow of doubt, the fact of Christ's

humanity; the name indicates the majesty of His glory. He
was circumcised because He was truly a son of Abraham; He
was called Jesus, that name that is above all names, because
He was truly the Son of God.

¶246 • _____ • **On the Love of God, Ch. 1** • You wish to hear
from me why and how God should be loved? I respond: the
reason for loving God is God Himself; the way is to love Him
beyond measure.

¶247 • **Peter Lombard (c. 1095 - 1160)** • **Sentence 4:2** • Let us now
come to the sacraments of the new covenant. They are
baptism, confirmation, the blessing of the bread which is the
Eucharist, penance, extreme unction, ordination, and
marriage.
    Of these, some offer a remedy for sin and confer helping
grace . . . others strengthen us with grace and virtue.

¶248 • _____ • **Sentences, 3:26** • Hope is the certain
expectation of future glory, the fruit of divine grace and
preceding merit.

¶249 • **Gratian (12th cent.)** • **Decretals of, D 8:13** • Natural law is
superior in dignity to customs and enactments. For whatever
has been received through usage or written down that is
contrary to natural law, is to be considered void and invalid.
    There can be no dispensation from the natural law, except
perhaps in the case of two evils when it is necessary to
choose one or the other.

¶250 • **Ivo of Chartres, St. †1115** • **Letter to Pope Paschal II** •
When kingdom and priesthood are at one, in complete
accord, the world is well-ruled and the Church flourishes and
brings forth abundant fruit. But when they are at variance,
not only do small interests suffer, but even things of the
greatest moment fall into deplorable decay.

¶**251** • **Thomas Becket, St. †1170** • **Letter 74** • The Roman Church remains the head of all the churches and the source of Catholic teaching. Of this there can be no doubt. Everyone knows that the keys of the kingdom of heaven were given to Peter.

Upon his faith and teaching the whole fabric of the Church will continue to be built until we all reach the full maturity in Christ and attain to unity in faith and knowledge of the Son of God.

All important questions that arise among God's people are referred to the Judgment of Peter in the person of the Roman Pontiff.

¶**252** • **Richard of St.-Victor †1173** • **On the Four Stages of Love** • I am wounded by love. Love urges me to speak of love. Gladly do I give myself up to the service of love, and it is sweet and altogether lovely to speak about love.

This is a joyful subject and very fruitful, one that will not weary the writer nor fatigue the reader. For that which savors of charity pleases the heart's taste beyond measure.

Above all, there is that ardent and burning love which penetrates the heart, inflames the affection, and transfixes the soul itself to the very core so that it may truly say, "I am wounded by love."

¶**253** • **Alain de Lille †1202** • **Parables** • A thousand roads lead men forever to Rome. . . . All is not gold that shines like gold.

¶**254** • **Peter Bloisius †c. 1212** • **Sermon to Priests, No. 60** • A priest has the primacy of Abel, the patriarchate of Abraham, the government of Noah, the order of Melchizedek, the dignity of Aaron, the authority of Moses, the perfection of Samuel, the power of Peter, the unction of Christ.

¶**255** • **Magna Charta (1215)** • **From No. 42, No. 43** • No freedman shall be arrested or detained in prison, or deprived of his freehold, or outlawed, or banished, or in any way molested, and we shall not set forth against him, nor send against him, unless by the lawful judgment of his peers and by the law of the land.

To no one will we sell, to no one will we refuse or delay, right or justice.

¶256 • **Innocent III, Pope †1216** • **Veni, Sancte Spiritus, v. 1** • Holy Spirit, come and shine / On our souls with beams divine / Issuing from Your radiance bright. / Come, O Father of the Poor, / Ever bounteous in Your store / Come, our heart's unfailing light.

¶257 • **Dominic, St. (c. 1170 - 1221)** • **Sermon in Languedoc** • For many years I have exhorted you in vain, with gentleness, preaching, praying, and weeping. But according to the proverb of my country, "Where blessing can accomplish nothing, blows may prevail." Must blows prevail where gentleness and blessings have been powerless?

¶258 • **Francis of Assisi, St. †1226** • **Canticle of the Sun, Introd.** • Most high, omnipotent, good Lord, / Praise, glory, honor, benediction, all are Thine. / To Thee alone do they belong, most High, / And there is no man fit to mention Thee. / Praise be to Thee, my Lord, with all Thy creatures, / Especially to my worshipful Brother Sun, / Which lights up the day, and through him dost Thou brightness give; / Beautiful is he and radiant with splendor great; / Of Thee, most High, signification gives.

¶259 • _____ • **Little Flowers** • Here is perfect joy: above all the grace and gifts of the Holy Spirit that Christ grants to His beloved are to overcome oneself and willingly, for the love of Christ, endure pains and insults and shame and want. In all the other gifts of God we may not glory, since they are not ours but God's, as the Apostle says, "What have you that you have not received?"

But in the cross of tribulation we may boast since it is ours, and therefore the Apostle says, "I do not glory save in the cross of our Lord Jesus Christ."

¶260 • _____ • **Prayer, attributed to him** • Make me, O Lord, an instrument of Your peace. / Where there is hatred, let me sow love; Where there is injury, pardon; / Where there is doubt, faith; / Where there is despair, hope; / Where there is darkness, light; / Where there is sadness, joy.

O Divine Master, grant that I may not so much seek to be consoled as to console, to be understood as to understand, to be loved as to love.

For it is in giving that we receive; it is in pardoning that we are pardoned; and it is in dying that we are born to eternal life. Amen.

¶261 • **Anthony of Padua, St. †1231** • **Sermon** • One who is filled with the Holy Spirit speaks in different languages. These different languages are different ways of witnessing to Christ, such as humility, poverty, patience, and obedience. We speak in these languages when we reveal, in ourselves, these virtues to others.

Actions speak louder than words; let your words teach and your actions speak.

¶262 • **Edmund of Abingdon, St. †1240** • **Prayer, v. 2** • Keep us, O Lord Jesus, through the day, by the merits and intercession of the Blessed Virgin Mary and all Your saints, from all vicious and unruly desires, from all sins and temptations of the devil, and from sudden and unprovided death and the pains of hell.

¶263 • **Durand, William, the Elder (13th cent.)** • **On Bells, Introd.** • Bells are brazen vessels that were first invented in Nola, a

city of Campania. Therefore, larger bells are called
Campanae, from Campania the district, and the smaller are
called *Nolae*, from Nola the town (and thus a major bell tower
is called a *Campanile*).

Bells symbolize the silver trumpets which in the Old Law
called the people together. They summon the people to
Church and the priests to preach "in the morning the Mercy
of God, and by night His power."

Our brazen bells are more sonorous than, more durable
than the trumpets of the Old Testament since they signify
that the New Testament will be more lasting, indeed, will last
to the end of time.

¶264 • **Louis IX, King, St. (13th cent.)** • **Instruction** • My son, if
you come to reign, do that which befits a king, that is, to be so
just as to deviate in nothing from justice, whatever might
happen to you. If a poor man goes to law with one who is
rich, support the poor rather than the rich until you know the
truth, and when the truth is known, do what is just.

¶265 • **Matthew Paris (13th cent.)** • **Major History, Introd.** • The
case of historical writers is hard, for if they tell the truth they
provoke men, and if they write what is false they offend God.

¶266 • **Marco Polo (13th cent.)** • **Travels** • On the north of
Armenia is found a fountain from which a liquor like oil
flows, which, though unprofitable for the seasoning of meat,
is good for burning and for anointing camels afflicted with the
mange. This oil flows constantly and copiously, so that the
camels are laden with it.

¶267 • **Romance of the Rose (13th cent.)** • Three cruel
vengeances pursue / Those miserable wretches who / Hoard
up their worthless wealth: great toil / Is theirs to win it; then
their spoil / They fear to lose; and lastly grieve / Most
bitterly that they must leave / Their hoards behind them.

Cursed they die / Who, living, lived but wretchedly; / For no man, if he lack of love, / Has peace below or joy above. . . .

¶268 • **Thomas of Celano** †c. 1260 • **Dies Irae, Dies Illa, vv. 1-3** • Day of wrath, that dreadful day, / When heaven and earth shall pass away, / Both David and the Sibyl say.

What terror then shall us befall / When lo! the Judge's steps appall, / Above to sift the deeds of all.

The mighty trumpet's marvelous tone / Shall pierce through each sepuchral stone / And summon all before the Throne.

¶269 • **Clare of Assisi, St.** †1253 • **Prayer** • I pray You, O most gentle Jesus, having redeemed me by Baptism from original sin, so now by Your Precious Blood, which is offered and received throughout the world, deliver me from all evils, past, present, and to come.

By Your most cruel death give me a lively faith, a firm hope, and perfect charity so that I may love You with all my heart and all my soul and all my strength; make me firm and steadfast in good works and grant me perseverance in Your service so that I may be able to please You always. Amen.

¶270 • **Richard of Chichester, St.** †1253 • **Day by Day** • Thanks be to You, My Lord Jesus Christ, for all the blessings and benefits which You have given me, for all the pains and insults You have borne for me.

O most merciful Friend, my Brother and Redeemer, may I know You more clearly, love You more dearly, and follow You more nearly, day by day, day by day. Amen.

¶271 • **Simon Stock, St.** †1265 • **Prayer** • O beautiful Flower of Carmel, most fruitful vine, Splendor of Heaven, holy and singular, who brought forth the Son of God, still ever remaining a pure Virgin, assist me in my necessities.

O Star of the Sea, help and protect me! Show me that you are my Mother. Amen.

¶272 • **Bonaventure, St. (c. 1217 - 1274)** • **Breviloquium, 1:i** • Since man could not have recovered excellence except through the most excellent Restorer, nor friendship except through the most friendly Mediator, nor purity of soul except through the most superabundant Satisfier; and the most excellent Restorer could be none other than God, the most friendly Mediator none but a man, the most superabundant Satisfier none but Him who was both God and man: therefore it was absolutely the most fitting thing for our restoration that the Word became incarnate.

¶273 • _____ • **Breviloquium, 6:3** • Because Baptism is for those entering the battle of life, Confirmation for those fighting, Holy Eucharist for those recuperating, Penance for those rising anew, Extreme Unction for those about to leave, Orders for those bringing in new recruits, and Matrimony for those providing these recruits — it is clear that the sacramental remedies and means of defense are sufficient and orderly.

¶274 • _____ • **Minor Works, No. 3** • It was a divine decree that permitted one of the soldiers to open His [Jesus'] side with a lance. The blood and water which poured out at that moment were the price of our salvation. Flowing from the secret abyss of our Lord's heart as from a fountain, this stream gave the sacraments of the Church the power to confer the life of grace, while for those already living in Christ it becomes a spring of living water welling up unto life eternal.

¶275 • **Thomas Aquinas, St. (1225 - 1274)** • **Commentary on Romans 2:4** • In Baptism, Christ's passion works a regeneration; a person dies entirely to the old life and takes on the new.

Therefore Baptism washes away the whole guilt of
punishment belonging to the past.

¶276 • _____ • **Minor Conferences, No. 2** • The first point
about eternal life is that man is united with God. God himself
is the reward and end of all of our labors. Next it consists in
perfect praise. It also consists in the complete satisfaction of
desire, for the blessed will be given more than they wanted or
hoped for. Again, eternal life consists in the joyous
community of all the blessed.

¶277 • _____ • **On John, No. 14** • If you are looking for the
way by which you should go, take Christ, because He himself
is the Way. It is better to limp along the way than stride
along off the way. For one who limps along the way, even if
he only makes slow progress, comes to the end of the way;
but one who is off the way, no matter how quickly he runs,
he ends up further from his goal.

¶278 • _____ • **Lauda Sion Salvatorem, v. 6** • And in faith
the Christian hears / That Christ's Flesh as bread
appears, / And as wine His Precious Blood; / Though we feel
it not nor see it, / Living faith indeed decrees it, / All defects
of sense makes good.

¶279 • _____ • **On the Feast of Corpus Christi** • Christ offered
His Body to God the Father on the altar of the cross as a
sacrifice for our reconciliation. He shed His Blood for our
ransom and purification, so that we might be redeemed from
our wretched state of bondage and cleansed from all sin.

He left His Body as food and His Blood as drink for the
faithful to consume in the form of bread and wine. . . .

It is offered in the Church for the living and the dead so
that what was instituted for the salvation of all may be for the
benefit of all.

¶280 • _____ • **Pange Lingua, vv. 4, 5** • Word made Flesh, the bread of nature / By His word to Flesh He turns. / Wine into His Blood He changes, / What though sense no change discerns? / Only be the heart in earnest, / Faith her lesson quickly learns.

Down in adoration falling, / Lo the sacred Host we hail! / Lo o'er ancient forms departing, / Newer rites of grace prevail! / Faith for all defects supplying / Where the feeble senses fail.

¶281 • _____ • **Summa Theologiae, I:13:8 ad 2** • We can name a thing according to the knowledge we have of its nature from its properties and effects. Hence, because we can know what stone is in itself from its property, this name, stone, signifies the nature of stone itself, for it signifies the definition of stone by which we know what it is, for the idea which the name signifies is the definition.

Now from the divine effects we cannot know the divine nature in itself, so as to know what it is, but only by way of eminence, and by way of causality and of negation. Thus, the name *God* signifies the divine nature, for this name was imposed to signify something existing above all things, the principle of all things, and removed from all things; for those who name God intend to signify all this.

¶282 • _____ • **Summa, 3:35:4** • To be conceived and to be born are attributed to the person (hypostasis) according to the nature conceived and born. Since a human nature was taken by a Divine Person in the very instant of conception, it follows that it can be said in actual truth that God was conceived and born of the Virgin. From this, a woman is called a man's mother, namely that she conceived him and gave birth to him.

Therefore, the Blessed Virgin Mary is truly called the Mother of God.

¶283 • _____ • **Summa, 3:73:5** • Because last words, especially such as are spoken by departing friends, are committed more deeply to memory, since then especially affection for friends is more enkindled, and the things which affect us most are impressed deepest in the soul, our Lord instituted this sacrament at His last parting with His disciples, in order that it might be held in the greater veneration.

¶284 • _____ • **Summa Contra Gentiles, Ch. 39** • From what has already been stated, it is clear according to the teachings of the Catholic Faith that we must say that in Christ there is a perfect divine nature and a perfect human nature, constituted by a rational soul and human flesh; and that these two natures are united in Christ not by indwelling only, nor in an accidental mode, as a man is united to his garments, nor in a personal relation and property only, but in one hypostasis and one supposit.

Only in this way can we save what the Scriptures hand on about the Incarnation. Sacred Scripture, without distinction, attributes the things of God to that man, and the things of that man to God; He of whom each class is said must be one and the same.

¶285 • **Albert the Great, St. †1280** • **Prayer** • "Fear not, Mary, for you have found grace with God" (Luke 1:30). Fear not, Mary, for you have found, not taken grace, as Lucifer tried to take it.

You have not lost it as Adam lost it. You have found it because you desired it and sought after it. You have found uncreated grace: that is, God Himself became your Son, and with that grace you have found and obtained every uncreated good. Amen.

¶286 • **Dante Alighieri (1265 - 1231)** • **Convivio, 4, v. 3** • When the immeasurable goodness of divine nature willed to restore

human nature to the image and likeness of God which had
been lost by the sin of Adam, it was decreed in the high and
united consistory of the Trinity that the Son of God should
come to earth to bring about this concord. And because at His
coming it was fitting that the earth should be in the most
perfect disposition, and because the world is at its best when
there is a world community, that is, when all are subject to a
single law, it was ordained by divine providence that the
people and the glorious city of Rome should be the means of
bringing this to pass.

And because it was proper that the inn where the
heavenly king was to rest should be immaculate, a holy race
was chosen in which, after the lapse of years, a woman above
all other women should be born to serve as the resting place
for the Son of God. The race was the race of David, and from
it sprang the boast and the glory of the human race, that is,
Mary.

¶287 • _____ • **Divine Comedy, Paradiso 5** • You have the
New Testament and the Old Testament, and the Shepherd of
the Church to guide you; let this be enough for your
salvation.

¶288 • _____ • **Divine Comedy, Purgatorio 15** • The infinite
and ineffable good that is God goes out toward proffered love
as a sunbeam meets a mirror. God gives himself in proportion
to the love He finds, so that however far our charity extends,
eternal power exceeds it.

¶289 • **Gertrude the Great, St. †1302** • **Prayer** • I salute you
through the Sacred Heart of Jesus, all you holy angels and
saints of God; I rejoice in your glory and I give thanks to Our
Lord for all the benefits which He has showered on you.

I praise Him and glorify Him and offer you, for an
increase of your joy and honor, the most gentle Heart of

Jesus. Deign, therefore, to pray for me so that I may become according to the Heart of God. Amen.

¶290 • **Boniface VIII, Pope †1303** • **Unam Sanctam** • Prompted by divine faith, we are obliged to believe and to hold that there is one holy, catholic, and apostolic Church, and this we firmly believe and simply confess . . . which constitutes one mystical Body, whose Head is Christ.

¶291 • **Jacopone da Todi †1306** • **Stabat Mater Dolorosa, vv. 1, 4** • At the Cross her station keeping, / Stood the mournful Mother weeping, / Close to Jesus to the last: / Through her heart His sorrow sharing, / All His bitter anguish bearing, / Now at length the sword has passed.

Bruised, derided, cursed, defiled, / She beheld her tender Child / All with bloody scourges rent; / For the sins of His own nation, / Saw Him hang in desolation, / Till His Spirit forth He sent.

¶292 • **John of Paris, O.P. †1306** • **Concerning Royal and Papal Power** • As in each diocese there is one bishop who is the head of the Church among that people, so in the whole Church and over all Christian people there is one supreme bishop, namely the Pope of Rome, successor to St. Peter, that the Church militant may bear the likeness of the Church triumphant where One presides over the whole universe. . . .

The priesthood is the spiritual power conferred on the ministers of the Church by Christ for the purpose of dispensing the sacraments to the faithful.

¶293 • **Eckhart, Meister, O.P. †1327** • **Book of Divine Consolation, Pt. 2** • There is no suffering or loss without some comfort, neither is there any loss that is sheer loss. Hence, St. Paul says that God's faithfulness and goodness do not allow any trouble to be unbearable.

He creates and bestows at all times some comfort of which

one can avail oneself, for the sacred and the pagan writers
also say that God and nature do not allow pure evil or pain to
exist.

¶ 294 • **Anon. (c. 1330)** • **Anima Christi** • Soul of Christ,
sanctify me. / Body of Christ, save me. / Blood of Christ,
inebriate me. / Water from the side of Christ, wash
me. / Passion of Christ, comfort me. / O good Jesus, hear
me. / Within Your wounds, hide me. / Never permit me to be
separated from You. / From the wicked enemy, defend
me. / In the hour of my death, call me / And bid me come to
You, / That with Your saints I may praise You / Forever and
ever. Amen.

¶ 295 • **Benedict XII, Pope †1342** • **Benedictus Deus** • The souls of
all the saints who departed from this world before the passion
of our Lord Jesus Christ, as also the souls of the holy
apostles, martyrs, confessors, virgins, and the rest of the
faithful who have departed this life after receiving Christ's
baptism, in whom there is found nothing calling for
purification when they died . . . even before the resurrection
of their bodies and the general judgment, have been, are, and
will be, since the Ascension of Our Lord, gathered into
heaven and have seen and do see the Divine Essence face to
face.

¶ 296 • **Rolle de Hampole, Richard (c. 1300 - 1349)** • If you would
be well with God and have grace to rule your life and come to
the joy of love, fix the name of "Jesus" so fast in your heart
that it is never out of your thoughts. . . . If you think "Jesus"
continually and hold it firmly, it purges your sins, kindles
your heart, cleanses the soul, removes anger, and does away
with sloth. It wounds in love and fulfills in charity. It opens
heaven and makes a man a contemplative.

¶297 • **Catherine of Siena, St. †1380** • **Letter to Monna Agnese** •
There is no sin nor wrong that gives a man such a foretaste of
hell in this life as anger and impatience.

¶298 • _____ • **On Divine Providence, No. 4** • Moved by love
and wishing to reconcile the human race to Yourself, You
gave us Your only-begotten Son. He became our Mediator
and our justice by taking on all our injustice and sin, out of
obedience to Your will, eternal Father, just as You willed that
He take on our human nature. What an immeasurably
profound love! Your son came down from the heights of His
divinity to the depths of our humanity. Can anyone's heart
remain closed and hardened after this?

¶299 • **Tauler, Johannes, O.P. †1361** • **Sermon 39** • Love attracts
all the good there is in heaven, in the angels and the saints
and all the sufferings of the martyrs. Furthermore, love
draws to itself all the good that is contained in all the
creatures in heaven and on earth, of which so much is lost, or
seems to be lost. It is love that keeps it from perishing. The
spiritual masters and the saints tell us that eternal life is filled
with a love that is exceedingly great.

¶300 • **Innocent VI, Pope (1325 - 1362)** • **Ave Verum Corpus Natum** •
Hail, true Body, truly born / Of the Virgin Mary
mild, / Truly offered, racked and torn, / On the cross for man
defiled. / From whose love-pierced, sacred side / Flowed
Your true Blood's saving tide. / Be a foretaste sweet to
me / In my death's great agony, / O You loving, gentle
One, / Sweetest Jesus, Mary's Son.

¶301 • **Bridget of Sweden, St. †1373** • **Revelations, prayer 2** •
Blessed are You, my Lord Jesus Christ. You foretold Your
death and at the Last Supper you marvelously consecrated
bread which became Your precious Body. And You gave it to
Your apostles out of love as a memorial of Your most holy

passion. By washing their feet with Your holy hands, You gave them a supreme example of humility.

¶302 • **Petrarch (Petrarca, Francesco) †1374** • **Canzone 16** • A good death does honor to a whole life.

¶303 • **Julian of Norwich (1342 - c. 1420)** • **Revelations** • God showed the very great pleasure He takes in all men and women who mightily and wisely receive the preaching and teaching of the Church. For He is Holy Church, He is its ground, its substance, its teaching. He is its Teacher. He is the end and the reward toward which every kind soul travels. . . .

By this vision He showed me how to grow in its teaching, that I might, by His grace, increase and rise to more heavenly knowledge and higher loving.

¶304 • **Hilton, Walter †1395** • **Scale of Perfection** • All other gifts of God and works of man are common to the good and the bad, to the elect and the reprobate, but the gift of charity belongs only to the good and to the elect. . . .

It is easier to renounce worldly possessions than it is to renounce the love of them.

¶305 • **Barbour, John †1395** • **The Bruce** • Ah! Freedom is a noble thing. / Freedom makes man to have liking: / Freedom all solace to man gives: / He lives at ease that freely lives.

¶306 • **Froissart, Jean (c. 1340 - c. 1405)** • **Passim** • The most profitable thing in the world for the instruction of human life is history.

¶307 • **Langland, William †1400** • **Piers Plowman, 8** • But there are seven sisters ever serving Truth, / Porters of the Postern; one called Abstinence, / Humility, Charity, Chastity be the chief maidens there; / Patience and Peace help many a one; / Lady Almsgiving lets in full many.

¶308 • **Chaucer, Geoffrey †1400** • **Canterbury Tales** • Whoso will pray, he must fast and be clean, / And fat his soul, and make his body lean. (*Somnoir [Summoner's Tale]* 1.171)

God, when He made the first woman, made woman of the rib of Adam, / For woman should be fellow unto man. (*Parson's Tale*, sec. 79)

¶309 • **Gower, John †1408** • **Confessio Amantis** • The fraile flesh whose nature is / Ay ready for the sporne and fall, / The first Foeman is of all. / It warreth night, it warreth day, / So that a man hath never rest. . . / For he who naught dare undertake, / By right he shall no profit take. . . / Who that well his work beginneth / The rather a good end he winneth. . . / The end proveth everything.

¶310 • **Gerson, John Charlier de †1429** • **Letter** • Though I have spent years in reading and prayer, yet I could never find anything more efficacious, nor, for attaining to mystical theology, more direct, than that the spirit should become like a little child, and a beggar, in the presence of God.

¶311 • **Bernardine of Siena, St. †1444** • **Sermon 2 On St. Joseph** • What is St. Joseph's position in the whole Church of Christ? Is he not a man chosen and set apart? Through him and, yes, under him, Christ was fittingly and honorably introduced into the world.

Holy Church in its entirety is indebted to the Virgin Mother because through her it was judged worthy to receive Christ. But after her we undoubtedly owe special gratitude and reverence to St. Joseph. God has adorned him with all the gifts of the Holy Spirit needed to fulfill his task.

¶312 • _____ • **On the Visitation** • The Mother and Mistress of Wisdom speaks few words, but each is filled with great depth of meaning. We read that the Mother of Christ spoke seven times, seven words filled with wisdom.

Twice she spoke to the angel and twice to Elizabeth. She also spoke to her Son twice, once in the Temple and once at the marriage feast. There she also spoke to the attendants.

On all these occasions she spoke very little, except for the one time when the praises of God just poured forth from her lips in thanksgiving. Then she said, "My soul magnifies the Lord. . . ."

¶313 • **Hoccleve, Thomas †1450** • **On the Rule of Princes** • The voice of the people is the voice of God, men say.

¶314 • **John of Capistrano, St. †1456** • **Mirror of the Clergy, No. 1** • It is indeed a double task that worthy priests perform, that is to say, it is both exterior and interior, both temporal and spiritual, and finally, both a passing task and an eternal one.

So it must be with the glowing lives of upright and holy clerics. By the brightness of their holiness they must bring light and serenity to all who look at them. Their own lives should be an example to others.

¶315 • **Thomas à Kempis (1380 - 1471)** • **The Imitation of Christ, 2:2, 3** • Do not care much who is with you and who is against you, but make it your greatest care to see that God is with you in everything you do.

Above all things keep peace within yourself, then you will be able to create peace among others. It is better to be a man of peace than a learned man.

If you wish others to put up with you, first put up with them.

¶316 • _____ • **Imitation of Christ, 2:10** • You have here no lasting city. For wherever you find yourself, you will always be a pilgrim from another city. Until you are united intimately with Christ, you will never find your true rest.

¶317 • **Denis (Dionysius) the Carthusian †1471** • **Homo Dei** • Creature of God, immortal man! / Poor vessel wrought to clay! / Whose present life is but a span, / So quick it fleets away.

¶318 • **Fortescue, John †1476** • **Government of England** • There are two kinds of kingdoms, one a lordship called in Latin *dominium regale*, and the other is called *dominium politicum et regale*. And they differ in that the first king may rule his people by such laws as he makes. The second king may not rule his people by other laws than such as they assent to themselves.

[6]
Renaissance and Counter-Reform

It was the worst of times, it was the best of times, as the master story-teller described another age. For those who loved the Church it was a time of tragedy when the seamless robe of Christ's Church was torn asunder.

Never since the time of the Arian heresy had so many souls been snatched away from the True Church. The work of men like Luther, Zwingli, Calvin, Knox, Melancthon, and the rest seemed like the work of the devil himself.

At first their work was dismissed as a quarrel among monks, and the occasion for it quite unworthy of all the trouble. The Catholic theologians dubbed them "the Innovators," since they were making doctrinal statements that had never before been accepted in the Christian Church.

It should be clear from the documents sampled so far in this book that statements like "the Bible alone," or "faith alone" are foreign to sixteen hundred years of Christianity. The substitution for the ordained priesthood of the priesthood of the laity simply has no historic or doctrinal basis.

But, as with some modern and bitter disputes that are masked behind religious differences (I think of Northern Ireland, Lebanon, South Africa, and other places), there were economic and political movements of vast urgency behind the religious questions.

The political winds that were fanning the flames of nationalism were perhaps more consciously at work in the sixteenth century than most modern writers believe. Later, Cardinal Richelieu would make an alliance with the Protestant Gustavus Adolphus to scourge his Catholic rivals.

English Protestants descended on Catholic Ireland like a plague of locusts.

The economic and financial interests were slower in emerging, but when the Industrial Revolution finally hit, the Catholic theologians and philosophers were aghast at the tremendous injustices wreaked on the poor to gain notorious wealth for the few. That was planted in the Protestant Reformation.

But so much for the worst of times. It also brought on the best of times. The Catholic Counter-Reform movement brought out the best in contemporary theologians, gave birth to a dynamic, reforming ecumenical council, the Council of Trent, and gave the Church several generations of outstanding saints.

Even those who loved the Church dearly during the fourteenth and fifteenth centuries recognized the slump in holiness and creative activity in the Church. There was a need for reform, and Martin Luther was so very right in his call for an overhaul. If Luther had left dogma alone and concentrated on the human abuses that grew ever stronger as the sixteenth century began, I am convinced that he would have emerged as a great reformer, hero, and saint of the Catholic Church.

On the human side, the Church that he envisioned emerged from Trent with a vigor that carried it along for more than two centuries, before the need for further "reform and renewal" began to be evident. It is concrete evidence of the activity of the Holy Spirit within the Church, and Christ's promise that the Spirit of Truth would be with the Church until the end of time.

In the context of all this theological growth and life, there were two whole new worlds opened to Europe — the Far East and the Western Hemisphere, comprising North and South America. The Church was soon winning whole new nations for Christ even as the northern European countries braced themselves into Protestantism.

Marco Polo's tales had been greeted with open skepticism, but now the evidence of souls to be won by the thousands and millions captured the imagination of the Church, and the great work of the missioners was on.

¶319 • **Joan of Valois, St.** †1505 • **The Ten Virtues of Our Lady** • O Virgin most patient, grant us patience amid the trials and sorrows so plentiful in this world, so that after the storm of adversities, afflictions, and anguish which everywhere assail us, we may with joy reach the land of the living, the haven of eternal beatitude, there to enjoy the everlasting rest prepared for the elect.

¶320 • **Francis of Paola, St.** †1507 • **Letters** • Fix your minds on the passion of our Lord Jesus Christ. Consumed with love for us, He descended from heaven to redeem us. For our sake, He endured every torment of body and soul and He shrank from no bodily pain. He himself gave us the perfect example of patience and love. Therefore, we are to be patient in adversity.

¶321 • **Everyman (mystery play, anon.), c. 1525** • God: Where art thou, Death, thou mighty messenger?
Death: Almighty God, I am here at Your will, / Your commandment to fulfill.

¶322 • **Wolsey, Thomas, Cardinal** †1530 • **Last Words** • Had I but served God as diligently as I have served my king, he would not have given me over in my grey hairs. But this is the just reward for my indulgent pains and study, not regarding my service to God, but only to my prince.

¶323 • **Cajetan (Gaetano), Giacomo, Cardinal, St.** †1547 • **Commentary on the Summa, 2, 2, 81.8** • Religion is directly concerned with those things which specially pertain to divine worship — ceremonies, for example, sacrifices, oblations, etc. Whereas sanctity directly regards the mind and through the mind the other virtuous works, including those of religion, for it makes use of them so as thereby to apply the mind — and by consequence all acts that proceed from the human mind — to God. Thus we see that many religious people are not saints, whereas all saints are religious.

¶324 • **John Fisher, St. †1535** • **On Psalm 129** • Our high priest is Jesus Christ; our sacrifice is His precious Body, which He immolated on the altar of the cross for the salvation of all mankind.

The Blood that was poured out for our redemption was not that of goats or calves — as in the Old Law — but that of the most innocent Lamb, Jesus Christ our Savior.

¶325 • **Thomas More, St. (1478 - 1535)** • **Apology** • The Church was gathered and the faith was believed before ever any part of the New Testament was put in writing. And what writing was or is the true Scripture is known by the work of the Church — even Luther and Tyndale must believe that.

Why then should they not believe the Church when it tells them what Christ and the Apostles said and did, as they believe the Church when it tells them what the evangelists and apostles wrote?

¶326 • _____ • **Prison Letter** • By the merits of His bitter passion joined to mine and far surpassing in merit for me all that I can suffer myself, His bounteous goodness shall release me from the pains of purgatory and shall increase my reward in heaven besides.

¶327 • **Erasmus, Desiderius (c. 1466 - 1536)** • **The Militant Christian, No. 2** • If your interest in sacred doctrine revolves more about what is vital and dynamic rather than the merely dialectical, if you incline more toward what moves the inner man than what leads to empty arguments, then read the Fathers. Their deep piety has withstood the test of time. Their very thoughts constitute a prayerful meditation, and they penetrate into the very depths of the mysteries they propound.

¶328 • **Angela Merici, St.** †1540 • **Spiritual Testament** • Our Savior says, "A good tree is not able to produce bad fruit." A good tree, that is, a good heart as well as a soul inflamed with charity, can do nothing but good and holy works.

For this reason St. Augustine said, "Love God and do what you will," namely, possess love and charity and then do what you will. It is as if he said, "Charity is not able to sin."

¶329 • **Osuna, Francisco de** †1542 • **Third Spiritual Alphabet** • For once we have learned by faith that God is to be desired and loved and is wholly love — then if our affections be purged and prepared and exercised, I know not how we shall be hindered from being thus transformed, inflamed, and raised to a state which knows all to be one clod, one fragment, or, to speak better, one fount of love.

¶330 • **Laredo, Bernardino de** †1540 • **Ascent of Mt. Zion** • So often does our Lord and loving Physician visit the soul, which is faint for His love, that the soul reaches a point at which it cannot and would not escape the arrows of love, never lacking the Physician who with a glance heals it.

And this He does so completely that the soul has but to cry out of a sudden concerning its grievous sickness, and straightway it has its remedy, and the visit of the beloved Physician. No sooner is it afflicted with love than with the affliction it has the remedy.

¶331 • **Trent, Council of (1545 - 1563)** • **Sess. 2, Ch. 2 (1546)** • In things of faith and morals belonging to the building up of Catholic doctrine, that is to be considered the true sense of Holy Scripture which has been held and is held by our holy mother the Church, whose place it is to judge of the true sense and the interpretation of the Scriptures, and, therefore . . . it is permitted to no one to interpret Holy Scripture against such sense or also against the unanimous agreement of the Fathers.

¶332 • _____ • **Sess. 6, Canon 14 (1547)** • The Lord instituted the Sacrament of Penance when, on being raised from the dead, He breathed upon His disciples and said, "Whose sins you shall forgive, they are forgiven; whose sins you shall retain, they are retained."

¶333 • _____ • **Catechism No. 1 (c. 1550)** • This Church has but one ruler and one governor, the invisible one, Christ, whom the eternal Father has made head over all the Church, which is His Body (Eph. 1:22); the visible one who, as the legitimate successor of Peter the prince of the Apostles, fills the apostolic chair. That this visible head is necessary to establish and preserve unity in the Church is the unanimous accord of the Fathers.

¶334 • **John of God, St. †1550** • **Letter** • If we look forward to receiving God's mercy, we can never fail to do good as long as we have the strength. For if we share with the poor, out of the love of God, whatever He has given us, we shall receive according to His promise a hundredfold in eternal happiness. What a fine profit, what a blessed reward! Who would not entrust his possessions to this best of merchants who handles our affairs so well?

Just as water extinguishes fire, so love wipes away sins.

¶335 • **Francis Xavier, St. (1506 - 1552)** • **O Deus Ego Amo Te vv. 1, 5** • O God, I love You, not because / I hope for heaven thereby, / Nor yet since they who love You not / Must burn eternally.

E'en so I love You and will love, / And in Your praise will

sing, / Solely because You are my God, / And my eternal King.

¶336 • **Ignatius Loyola, St. (1491 - 1556)** • **Letter to St. Francis Borgia** • Learning will always be necessary, or certainly useful, and not only that which is infused, but that also which is acquired by study. . . . Try to keep your soul always in peace and quiet, always ready for whatever our Lord may wish to work in you.

It is certainly a more lofty virtue of the soul, and a greater grace, to be able to enjoy the Lord in different duties and places than in only one. We should, in the divine Goodness, make a great effort to attain this.

¶337 • _____ • **Spiritual Exercises, No. 2** • In order better to imitate Christ our Lord and to become actually more like Him, I desire and choose poverty with Christ — poverty, rather than riches; reproaches with Christ — laden with them, rather than honors; and I desire to be accounted as worthless and a fool for Christ, who was first held to be such, rather than wise and prudent in this world.

¶338 • _____ • **Spiritual Exercises, No. 4** • Man was created to praise, honor, and serve God. We therefore no more prefer health to sickness, riches to poverty, honor to disdain, long life to short, but desire and choose only that which more surely conduces toward the end for which we were created.

¶339 • **Charles V, Emperor †1558** • **Letter to the English Ambassador** • If we had been master of such a servant [St. Thomas More], of whose doing we ourselves have had these years no small experience, we would rather have lost the best city of our dominions, than have lost such a worthy counsellor.

¶340 • **Peter of Alcántara, St. †1562** • **Treatise on Prayer and Meditation** • Meditation seeks, contemplation finds; the one

chews its food, the other tastes it; the one reasons and
considers, the other is content with nought but looking upon
things, since already it has the taste and the love for them. In
short, the one is a means and the other an end; the one is a
path and a movement, the other is the end of this path, and
yet it is movement.

¶341 • **Grimald, Nicholas †1562** • **Of Friendship** • Of all the
heavenly gifts that mortal men commend, / What trusty
treasure in the world can countervail a friend?
　　O friendship, flower of flowers, O lovely sprite of life, / O
sacred bond of blissful peace, the stalwart staunch of strife.

¶342 • **Michelangelo Buonnarroti †1564** • **Writings** • Heaven-
born, the soul a heavenward course must hold; beyond the
world she soars; the wise man, I affirm, can find no rest in
that which perishes, nor will he lend his heart to anything
that depends on time.

¶343 • **Blois, Louis de, Bl. †1566** • **A Short Rule** • True devotion
is nothing else than good will by which a man holds himself
ready for all that concerns the worship, honor, and good
pleasure of God. . . .
　　Whoever desires to please God, to make any progress in
the spiritual life, and at length to arrive at perfection, must as
a first step detest all heresies and schisms, adhering firmly to
the Church Catholic, and subjecting himself humbly to her.

¶344 • **Las Casas, Bartolomé de (1474 - 1566)** • **The Destruction of the
Indies** • [The people of the Caribbean] are of a clean,
unspoiled, and vivacious intellect, very capable, and
receptive to every good doctrine; most prompt to accept our
Holy Catholic Faith, to be endowed with virtuous customs;
and they have as little difficulty with such things as any
people created by God in the world.
　　Once they have begun to learn of matters pertaining to

faith, they are so importunate to know them, and in frequenting the sacraments and divine service of the Church, that, to tell the truth, the clergy need to be endowed by God with preeminent patience to serve them.

¶345 • **John of Avila, Bl. †1569** • **Letter** • One act of thanksgiving, when things go wrong with us, is worth a thousand thanks when things are agreeable to our inclinations.

¶346 • _____ • **Spiritual Epistles** • He [God] would like to consume us, that our old man being destroyed, which is in the likeness of Adam, our new man may be born through love, which is the image of Christ. He would like to melt our hard hearts, to the end that, as on metal that is molten by heat the image willed by the artificer may be imprinted, so we, softened by love which causes us to melt as we hear the voice of the Beloved, may be without resistance, and ready for Christ to imprint upon us the image He wills — that is, the image of Christ himself, which is the image of love.

¶347 • **Heywood, John †c. 1579** • **Proverbs** • The crow thinks her own birds fairest in the world. / Beggars should not be choosers. / The best is best cheap. / It is better to bow than to break. / Many hands make light work. / As good play for nought as work for nought. / It hurts not the tongue to give fair words. / A woman has nine lives, like a cat. / He that never climbed, never fell. / A penny for your thought. / What shall be, shall be. / Two heads are better than one. / Mad as March hare. / They do not love who do not show their love.

¶348 • **Campion, Edmund, St. †1581** • **Letter to the Council (Campion's Brag)** • Be it known to you that we have made a league, all the Jesuits in the world, cheerfully to carry the cross you lay upon us, and never to despair your recovery, while we have a man left to enjoy your Tyburn, or to be racked with your torments, or consumed with your prisons.

The expense is reckoned, the enterprise begun; it is of God, it cannot be withstood. So the Faith was planted: so it must be restored.

¶349 • **Teresa of Avila, St. †1582** • **Bookmark** • Let nothing disturb you, / Let nothing frighten you. / All things are passing. / God alone does not change. / Patience achieves everything. / Whoever has God lacks nothing. / God alone suffices.

¶350 • _____ • **Interior Castle, 7th Mansion 4:9** • I insist, again, your foundation must not consist of prayer and contemplation alone. Unless you acquire the virtues and practice them, you will always be dwarfs.

¶351 • _____ • **The Way of Perfection, Ch. 22** • Before we begin reciting the Hours or the Rosary, we should think whom we are going to address, and who we are that are addressing Him, so that we may do so in the way we should.

I assure you that if you give all due attention to a consideration of these two points before beginning vocal prayers which you are about to say, you would be engaging in mental prayer for a very long time.

¶352 • **Charles Borromeo, St. (1538 - 1584)** • **Pastoral Letter** • In her concern for our salvation, our loving mother the Church uses the liturgical seasons to teach us through hymns, canticles, and other forms of expression, of voice and ritual, used by the Holy Spirit. She shows us how grateful we should be for our blessings.

¶353 • _____ • **Synodal Homily** • If teaching and preaching is your job, then study diligently and apply yourself to whatever is necessary for doing the job well. Be sure that you first preach by the way you live. If you do not, people will notice that you say one thing but live otherwise.

Are you in charge of a parish? If so, do you neglect the parish of your own soul? You have to be mindful of your people without becoming forgetful of yourself.

For us churchmen, nothing is more necessary than meditation. Meditate before, during, and after everything you do.

¶354 • _____ • **Third Provincial Council, No. 1** • Pastors and preachers should take every possible opportunity to urge the people to cultivate the practice of frequently receiving Holy Communion. In this they are following the example of the early Church, the recommendations of the most authoritative Fathers, the doctrine of the Roman Catechism, and finally the preaching of the Council of Trent. This last would have the faithful receive Holy Communion in every Mass, not only spiritually but sacramentally.

¶355 • **Mary Stuart, Queen of Scots †1567** • **Prayer for Generosity** • Keep me, O God, from pettiness. / Let us be large in thought, word and deed. / Let us be done with fault-finding and leave off self-seeking. / May we put away all pretense and meet each other face to face without self-pity and without prejudice. / And, O Lord God, / Let us not forget to be kind. Amen.

¶356 • **Luís de Granada †1588** • **Sinners' Guide** • Accordingly, when a man in this mortal life reaches so high a degree of love that he despises all things which perish, taking unlawful content of pleasure in none, but fixing all his pleasure, love, care, desire, and thought upon God, and this so constantly that always, or almost always, his heart is set on Him (for in Him alone he finds rest, and apart from Him none); when in this way a man is dead to all things, and alive only to God, the greatness of his love triumphing over all other affections, then he will have entered the vaults of precious wine of the true Solomon, in which, inebriated with the wine of love, he will forget all things, even himself, for His sake.

¶357 • **Sixtus V, Pope †1590** • **Triumphantis Jerusalem** • In writing, he [St. Bonaventure] united to the highest erudition an equal amount of the most ardent piety, so that while enlightening his readers he also touched their hearts, penetrating to the inmost recesses of their souls.

¶358 • **John of the Cross, St. †1591** • **Ascent of Mt. Carmel, 1:4, 2** • The reason, as we learn in philosophy, is that two contraries cannot coexist in the same subject. Darkness, an attachment to creature, and light, which is God, are contraries and bear no likeness to each other.
　　The light of divine Union cannot be established in the soul until these affections are eradicated.

¶359 • _____ • **Maxims** • Where there is no love, put love in and you will draw love out.

¶360 • _____ • **On Love, No. 78** • Never take a man for your example in the tasks you have to perform, however holy he may be. Imitate Christ, who is supremely perfect and supremely holy, and you will never err.

¶361 • **Allen, William, Cardinal †1594** • **Apology** • No earthly commonwealth can give or confer supremacy over the Church to the prince, because they cannot give that which they have not by any natural faculty.

¶362 • **Robert Southwell, St. †1595** • **Love's Precious Mark** • Love's precious mark, highest theme of praise; most desired light for man. / To love Him is life; to leave Him death; to live in Him and for Him, delight. / He is mine by gift; I am His by

debt; thus each to the other as meet. / He was my first
Friend; He is my best Friend; all things prove Him true. . . .

¶363 • Peter Canisius, St. (1521 - 1597) • On the Virgin Mother of God
• Why did the Fathers of the Church call the Virgin Mary by
the title "Queen"? They recognized the tremendous praise
heaped on her in the Scriptures. She is singled out as having
a King for her father, noble David, and the King of Kings and
Lord of Lords for her Son, whose reign will never end. . . .

There is not one who excels her in dignity, beauty or
holiness. Only the Holy Trinity is above her; all others are
below her in dignity and beauty.

**¶364 • Antoniano, Silvio Cardinal (1540 - 1603) • Fortem Virile
Pectore, vv. 1, 2 •** High let us all our voices raise, / In each
heroic woman's praise / Whose name, with saintly glory
bright, / Shines in the starry realms of light.

Filled with a pure celestial glow, / She spurned all love of
things below; / And heedless here on earth to stay, / Climbed
to the skies her toilsome way.

¶365 • Mary Magdalen dei Pazzi, St. †1607 • Prayer • Come,
Holy Spirit. Let the precious pearl of the Father and the
Word's delight come.

Spirit of truth, You are the reward of the saints, the
comforter of souls, light in darkness, riches to the poor,
treasure to lovers, food for the hungry, comfort to the
wanderer: You are the one in whom all treasures are
contained.

¶366 • Alphonsus Rodriguez, St. †1617 • Description of Mysticism •
Then the soul loves God and enjoys Him, because it is so
absorbed and, as it were, bathed in the divine love. The state
at which it has arrived is that of a very perfect union with
God, and, so to speak, of a transformation into God. At this
point, each gives to the other all he has and all he is.

¶367 • **Suárez, Francisco †1617** • **On the Angels, 6:4.16** • With regard to the most excellent Virgin Mary, as the Church herself sings, she is exalted above all the choirs of angels in the heavenly kingdom. It is certain that among all creatures, no matter how pure, the Blessed Virgin exceeds all in beatitude, even the angels.

Furthermore, it is exceedingly probable that even though she alone is superior to all in essential beatitude, a few of the saints may be equal to the highest orders of angels in perfection. In general, though, we can say that angels are higher than men.

¶368 • **Cervantes Saavedra, Miguel de †1616** • **Don Quixote** • When God dawns, He dawns for all (4:4). . . . God who gives the wound gives the salve (2:19). . . . God helps everyone with what is his own (2:26). . . . He who lives well is the best preacher (2:19). . . . Take away the motive, and sin is taken away (2:67).

¶369 • **Lawrence of Brindisi, St. †1619** • **Lenten Homily 2** • The word of God is a light to the mind and a fire to the will. It enables man to know God and to love Him. For the interior man who lives by the Spirit of God through grace, it is bread and water, but a bread sweeter than honey and the honeycomb, a water that is better than wine and milk. For the soul it is a spiritual treasure of merits yielding an abundance of gold and precious stones.

¶370 • **Robert Bellarmine, St. †1621** • **On the Church** • The one and true Church is the community of men brought together by the profession of the same Christian faith and conjoined in the communion of the same sacraments, under the government of the legitimate pastors and especially the one vicar of Christ on earth, the Roman Pontiff.

¶371 • _____ • **Pater Superni Luminis, vv. 1, 2** • Father in lights! one glance of Yours, / Whose eyes the universe control, / Fills Magdalen with holy love, / And melts the ice within her soul.

Her precious ointment forth she brings, / Upon those sacred feet to pour. / She washes them with burning tears, / And with her hair she wipes them o'er.

¶372 • **Francis de Sales, St. (1567 - 1622)** • **Introduction to the Devout Life, No. 1** • When God the Creator made all things, He commanded the plants to bring forth each according to its own kind; He has also commanded Christians, who are the living plants of His Church, to bring forth fruits of devotion, each one in accord with his own character, station, and calling.

The practice of devotion must be adapted to the strength, the occupation, and the duties of each one in particular.

True devotion embellishes and enhances each calling or occupation.

¶373 • _____ • **Introduction to the Devout Life, No. 30** • Do not fear what may happen tomorrow. The same loving Father who cares for you today will care for you tomorrow and every day.

Either He will shield you from suffering or He will give you unfailing strength to bear it.

Be at peace then, and put aside all anxious thoughts and imaginings.

¶374 • **Bérulle, Pierre de †1629** • **Thoughts** • Thus God incomprehensible makes Himself comprehended in this humanity; God ineffable makes Himself heard by the voice of His incarnate Word; God invisible shows Himself through the Flesh united by Him with the nature of eternity. O Miracle! O Glory!

¶375 • **Jane Frances de Chantal, St.** †**1641** • **Memoirs*** • There is another type of martyrdom, the martyrdom of love. Here God keeps His servants present in this life so that they may labor for Him, and He makes them martyrs and confessors as well.

Divine loves takes its sword to the hidden recesses of our inmost soul and divides us from ourselves. I know one person whom love cut off from all that was dearest to her, just as completely and effectively as if a tyrant's blade had severed spirit from body. [*Recorded by Mother Françoise-Madeleine de Chaugy.]

¶376 • **Baker, David Augustine** †**1641** • **Sancta Sophia** • Never did any spiritual mystical writer pretend to receive any new or formerly unknown lights or revelations in matters of faith or morals, beyond what have been clearly known and universally received in the Church. But they have a clearer sight of ordinary mysteries.

¶377 • **Galileo Galilei** †**1642** • **Authority of Scripture** • It is surely harmful to souls to make it a heresy to believe what is proved.

¶378 • **Urban VIII, Pope (1568 - 1644)** • **Regis Superna Nuntia, vv. 1, 2** • God's messenger, Teresa, / You left your father's home / To bring mankind to Jesus / Or gain sweet martyrdom.

But milder death awaits you, / And fonder pains are thine, / God's blessed angel wounds you / With fire of love divine.

¶379 • **Isaac Jogues, St.** †**1646** • **Last Letters*** • I shall go, but I shall not return. It will be a happiness for me, if God will be pleased to complete the sacrifice there where He began it. [*Ed. note: St. Isaac Jogues was martyred at Ossernon, near the present Utica, N.Y. on Oct. 18, 1646, about three months

after he wrote this. It was where he had be
four years earlier.]

¶380 • **Joseph Calasanz, St. †1648 • On Teacl**
undertake teaching must be endowed witl
greatest patience, and, most of all, profou
must perform their work with earnest zeal, that, through
their humble prayers, the Lord will find them worthy to
become fellow workers with Him in the cause of truth. He
will console them in the fulfillment of this most noble duty,
and finally He will enrich them with the gift of heaven.

¶381 • **Crashaw, Richard †1649 • To Our Lord on the Choice of His
Sepulcher** • How life and death in Thee / Agree! / Thou hadst a
virgin womb / And tomb. / A Joseph did betroth / Them
both.

¶382 • **John de Brébeuf, St. (1593 - 1649) • Instructions to
Missionaries (1637)** • Leaving a highly civilized community, you
fall into the hand of barbarous people who care little about
your philosophy or theology. All the fine qualities which
might make you loved in France are like pearls trampled
under the feet of swine, or rather of mules, which utterly
despise you when they see that you are not as good pack
animals as they are.

¶383 • **Charles I, King of England †1649 • On the scaffold** • I go
from a corruptible to an incorruptible crown, where no
disturbance can have place.

¶384 • **Descartes, René †1650 • Principles of Philosophy** • Our
idea of God implies necessary and eternal existence; the
manifest conclusion, then, is that God does exist.

¶385 • **Camus, Jean Pierre †1652 • The Spirit of St. Francis de Sales**
• He who believes himself to be far advanced in the spiritual

as not even made a good beginning. . . . The world is a eat stage on which God displays His many wonders. . . . One ounce of patient suffering is worth far more than a pound of action. . . . It is better to remain silent than speak the truth ill-humoredly, and so spoil an excellent dish by covering it with a bad sauce. . . . Love virtue rather than fear sin. . . . We must make use of this world as though we were not making use of it at all.

¶386 • **Habington, William †1654** • **Nox Nocti Indicat** • When I survey the bright / Celestial sphere, / So rich with jewels hung, that night / Doth like an Ethiope bride appear: / My soul her wings doth spread / And heavenward flies, / The Almighty's mysteries to read / In the large volume of the skies.

¶387 • **Vincent de Paul, St. †1660** • **Letters** • It is our duty to prefer service to the poor to everything else and to offer such service as quickly as possible. If a needy person requires medicine or other help during prayer time, do whatever has to be done with peace of mind. Offer the deed to God as your prayer.

Do not become upset or feel guilty because you interrupted prayer to serve the poor. God is not neglected if you leave Him for such service. One of God's works is merely interrupted so that another can be carried out. Charity is certainly greater than any rule.

¶388 • **Pascal, Blaise †1662** • **Pensées** • The serene, silent beauty of a holy life is the most powerful influence in the world, next to the might of the Holy Spirit. . . . One of the greatest artifices the devil uses, to engage men in vice and debauchery, is to fasten names of contempt on certain virtues, and thus fill weak souls with a foolish fear of passing for scrupulous, should they desire to put them into practice.

¶ 389 • **Davenant, Sir William †1668** • **Gondibert** • Ambition is the mind's immodesty. . . . Nor think ambition wise because 'tis brave. . . . Books: the monument of vanished minds which time does still disperse but not devour. . . . Truth: the discovery made by traveling minds.

¶ 390 • **Pius V, Pope St. †1672** • **Prayer to Christ Crucified, Nos. 1, 2** • Jesus Christ Crucified, Son of the most holy Virgin Mary! Incline Your Sacred Heart and listen to my petitions and sighs, as You listened to Your eternal Father on Mt. Tabor.

Jesus Christ Crucified, Son of the most holy Virgin Mary! Open Your Sacred Eyes and look on me as You looked on Your holy Mother from the cross.

¶ 391 • **John Eudes, St. †1680** • **On the kingdom of Jesus, No. 4** • Christ desires us to perfect the mystery of His Incarnation and birth by forming Himself in us and being reborn in our souls through the blessed sacraments of Baptism and the Eucharist. He fulfills His hidden life in us, hidden with Him in God.

¶ 392 • **Claude de la Colombière, Bl. †1682** • **Prayer** • O Jesus, You are my true Friend, my only Friend. You take part in all my misfortunes; You take them upon Yourself; You know how to change them into blessings.

You listen to me with greater kindness when I relate my troubles to You, and You always have balm to pour on my wounds. I find You at all times; I find You everywhere; You never go away; If I have to change my dwelling, I find You wherever I go.

¶ 393 • **Margaret Mary Alacoque, St. †1690** • **Letter** • It seems to me that the Lord's earnest desire to have His Sacred Heart honored in a special way is directed toward renewing the effects of the Redemption in our souls.

From this divine Heart, three streams flow endlessly. The

first is the stream of mercy for sinners; the second is the stream of charity which helps all in need; the third stream sheds love and light for His friends who have attained some perfection.

¶394 • **Paschal Baylon, St. †1592** • **Prayer** • I desire to love You, my Lord, my Light, / my strength, my deliverer, my God and my All. / What have I in Heaven, O God, what do I want besides You on earth? / My spirit and my body languish with yearning for Your Majesty. / You are the God of my heart; You are my portion, my inheritance for eternity. Amen.

[7]

'Reason' and Revolutionary Times

The seeds of disunity and discord sown by the Protestant
Reformation came into full flower in the eighteenth and
nineteenth centuries. There were wars and rumors of war all
over the world.

The stage was set in 1701 when the War of the Spanish
Succession broke out. This was followed almost immediately
by the warlike activities of Charles XII of Sweden. France
and England were constantly at each other's throats, and
Russia was active on the other side of the continent.

The wars spilled over into the colonial empires, igniting
hostilities in Canada, British America, Spanish America, and
India. The English sometimes slaughtered the American
Indians, and sometimes used them as paid allies against the
French and Spanish settlers.

As the years went by, there were the exploits of Peter the
Great in Russia and Frederick the Great in Prussia. The
Muslim world also had its disputes, but it was gradually
falling back under the dominance of the great European
powers.

The American Revolution came as a shock to England,
but it was hardly more than a prelude to the horrors of the
French Revolution. "Reason Alone" was just as harsh a
mistress as "Faith Alone."

The Church, which once might have mediated many of
these disputes, was powerless to act. The popes of this era
were generally good and capable men, but the traditional
Catholic allies were racked with anticlericalism,
Freemasonry, and their own power squabbles. Even the
Catholic countries, which were so generous in funding the

missionary efforts, were unable or unwilling to help the Church as peacemaker.

Even more tragic, in the long-range damage to souls, was the misguided attempt to suppress the Jesuits. For almost a generation they were under Church ban, surviving only in Russia and a few isolated spots. When they did return, however, they quickly filled a void no other religious order could, and once again they became the front-line forces of the Church Militant.

Simón Bolívar was the George Washington of the new countries in Latin America, but he was not able to bind them together into a union such as the United States, and so these countries, for the most part, still have to live up to their future.

Napoleon Bonaparte figures large at the middle of this period, and the latter part of it saw the inception of Communism, with its Marxist and atheistic philosophy.

On the missionary front, the Church succeeded almost beyond its dreams. Franciscans, Dominicans, Augustinians, every major religious order — and most of the minor ones — were represented around the world, reaping the harvest of souls.

In the United States, Bishop John Carroll, an ex-Jesuit, became the first English-speaking bishop in the present territory of this country. In Mexico and Peru and many other countries, there had been bishops, universities, and printing presses for more than two centuries. But the Church in Latin America was also to suffer much at the hands of the anticlericals and the Freemasons.

The wave of immigrants that swept into the United States in the last half of the nineteenth century gave the Church a strong voice and a powerful influence. The bishops of that time were a breed set apart, men of bricks and mortar who labored mightily for their immigrant flocks.

In England, Newman could announce a "Second Spring"

for the Church, and there was a great renaissance of Catholic art and letters.

A vigorous Church emerged from the crosses and trials of the period.

¶395 • **Dryden, John †1700** • **Absolom and Achitophel** • Bankrupt of life, yet prodigal of ease!

¶396 • _____ • **Annus Mirabilis** • The first happiness of the poet's imagination is properly invention, or finding of the thought; the second is fancy, or molding of that thought as the judgment represents it proper to the subject; the third is elocution, or the art of clothing and adorning that thought so found and varied, in apt, significant, and sounding words.

¶397 • _____ • **The Unhappy Favorite, Prologue** • When first the ark was landed on the shore, / And heav'n had vowed to curse the ground no more, / When tops of hills the longing patriach saw, / And the new scene of earth began to draw, / The dove was sent to view the waves' decrease, / And first brought back to man the pledge of peace.

¶398 • **Bossuet, Jacques Bénigne (1627 - 1704)** • **Panegyrics of the Saints: St. Paul** • The Divine Empire of the Church is founded on charity. This charity can take all sorts of different forms. It commands in pastors; it obeys in the people; but whether it commands or whether it obeys, it ever retains its characteristic properties: it is always charity, always gentle, always tender and sympathetic; never proud or ambitious.

Ecclesiastical government, then, being based upon and supported by charity, has nothing in it of domineering or overbearing; its commands are reasonable, its authority calm and sweet. . . . It guides and orders men with all the wise discretion of a far-reaching, fraternal love.

¶399 • **Fénelon, François †1715** • **Thoughts** • Peace does not dwell in outward things, but within the soul; we may preserve it in the midst of the bitterest pain, if our will remains firm and submissive. Peace in this life springs from acquiesence, not in the exemption of suffering. . . .

True piety has in it nothing weak, nothing sad, nothing constrained. It enlarges the heart; it is simple, free, and attractive.

¶400 • **Grignon de Montfort, Louis, St. †1716** • **On the Hail Mary** • Hail Mary, Daughter of God the Father! Hail Mary, Mother of God the Son! Hail Mary, Spouse of the Holy Spirit! Hail Mary, Temple of the Most Holy Trinity!

. . . Place yourself, O faithful Virgin, as a seal on my heart, that in you and through you I may be found faithful to God. Grant, most gracious Virgin, that I may be numbered among those whom you are pleased to love, to teach, and to guide, to favor and to protect as your children.

¶401 • **Garth, Sir Samuel †1719** • **The Dispensary** • Restless anxiety, forlorn despair, / And all the faded family of care. . . / Conquest pursues where courage leads the way. . . .

To die is landing on some silent shore, / Where billows never break, nor tempest roar; / Ere well we feel the friendly stroke, 'tis o'er, / As distant prospects please us, but when there, / We find but desert rocks and fleeting air.

¶402 • **John Baptist de la Salle, St. †1719** • **Prayer for Teachers** • You, O Lord, are my strength, my patience, my light and my counsel. It is You who make the children confided to my care attentive to me. Do not abandon me for one moment.

For my own conduct and for that of my pupils, grant me the spirit of wisdom and understanding, the spirit of counsel and fortitude, the spirit of knowledge and piety, the spirit of holy fear of the Lord, and an ardent zeal to promote Your glory.

I unite my labors with those of Jesus Christ, and I beg the most blessed Virgin, St. Joseph, and the Guardian Angels to protect me in the exercise of my employment.

¶403 • **Palumbella, Callisto †1720** • **O Quot Undis, vv. 1, 2** • What a sea of tears and sorrow / Did the soul of Mary toss / To and fro upon its billows / While she wept her bitter loss; / In her arms her Jesus holding, / Torn so newly from the cross.

Oh, that mournful Virgin Mother! / See her tears, how fast they flow / Down upon His mangled body, / Wounded side, and thorny brow; / While His hands and feet she kisses, / Picture of immortal woe.

¶404 • **Benedict XIV, Pope †1758** • **Ubi Primum** • It is of the utmost importance that you entrust the care of souls to exemplary men who are conspicuous for their doctrine, piety, purity, and good works. They should truly be and should be considered the light and the salt of the people.

These men are your principal aides in forming the flock entrusted to your care, governing it, purifying it, leading it in the path of salvation, and encouraging it to Christian virtue.

You should choose as parish priests men who may be judged suitable to the fruitful direction of people. Concentrate on this matter above everything else.

¶405 • **Crescentia Höss, Bl. †1744** • **Prayer** • O Lord, only grant me love for You and I shall be rich enough. I desire only that You leave me to my nothingness and that You alone, if I may say so, be all in all and loved and honored by everyone. I wish to take pleasure in nothing but only in You and in Your love. Amen.

¶406 • **Pope, Alexander †1744** • **An Essay on Man, No. 3** • In faith and hope the world will disagree, / But all mankind's concern is charity.

¶407 • **Ricchini, Augustine †1779** • **Coelestis Aulae Nuntius, vv. 1, 2** • The Messenger from God's high throne, / His secret counsel making known, / Hails Mary, child of David's race, / God's Virgin-Mother, full of grace.

The Mother-Maid with joyous feet / Her friend, John's mother, goes to greet. / He, stirring in th' enclosing womb, / Declares that Christ, his Lord, has come.

¶408 • **Clement XIII, Pope †1769** • **In Dominico Agro, No. 7 (1761)** • It is of the utmost importance that you choose, for the office of communicating Christian teaching to the faithful, not only men endowed with theological knowledge, but more importantly, men who manifest humility, enthusiasm for sanctifying souls, and charity.

¶409 • **Pius VI, Pope †1799** • **Inscrutabile, No. 4 (1775)** • A man who is going to be a priest should excel in holiness and learning. For God rejects as priests those who have rejected knowledge, and only the man who unites moral piety with the pursuit of knowledge can be a suitable worker in the Lord's harvest.

¶410 • **Serra, Fray Junípero (1713 - 1784)** • **Letter** • See to it that the new missionaries come well provided with patience, charity, and good temper, for they may find themselves rich in tribulations. But where can the laboring ox go that the plough will not be heavy to drag? And unless he drag it, how shall the seed be sown?

¶411 • _____ • **Letter (1776)** • Happy are they who have a son for a priest, who every day, in the Holy Sacrifice of the Mass, prays for them as best he can, and very often offers for them exclusively his Mass, so that the Lord sends them help.

¶412 • _____ • Nota Previa (1776) • The said Mission was first established near where at present the military camp or *presidio*, likewise called San Diego, is located. It was moved two leagues to the northeast to a place called in the native tongue *Nipaguay*. It was there that the devouring fire occurred.

The authors of that lamentable destruction were savages and perverted neophytes. . . . They pillaged part of it, burnt the greater portion, wounded a few resisting guards, and killed the blacksmith from Tepic, José Manuel Arroyo, and the carpenter from Guadalajara, José Urselino, and with untold cruelty, the principal and senior missionary, Rev. Father Lector Luís Jaime, who was a member of the Province of Majorca.

¶413 • Carroll, John, Bishop †1815 • Letter (1776) • I have observed that when ministers of religion leave the duties of their profession to take a busy part in political matters, they generally fall into contempt, and sometimes even bring discredit to the cause in whose service they are engaged.

¶414 • Alphonsus Liguori, St. (1696 - 1787) • The Glories of Mary: The Annunciation • God having determined to become man, that He might redeem lost souls, and thus show the world His infinite goodness, and having to choose a Mother on earth, He sought among all women the one that was the most holy and the most humble.

Among all of them there was one whom He admired, and this was the tender Virgin Mary, who, the more exalted by her virtues, so much the more dove-like was her simplicity and humility and the more lowly she was in her own estimation.

¶415 • **Benedict Joseph Labre, St. †1783** • **Reflections** • Jesus Christ, the King of Glory, came in peace. God was made man. The Word was made Flesh. Christ was born of the Virgin Mary. Christ walked in peace in the midst of people. Christ was crucified. Christ died. Christ was buried. Christ rose again. Christ ascended into heaven. Christ conquers, Christ reigns, Christ commands. May Christ defend us from all evil.

Jesus is with us!

¶416 • **Clement Mary Hofbauer, St. †1820** • **Prayer** • Remember Your mercies of old. Turn Your eyes in compassion upon the vineyard planted by Your own right hand, and watered by the tears of the Apostles, by the precious blood of countless martyrs, and made fruitful by the prayers of so many confessors and innocent virgins.

¶417 • **Seton, Elizabeth Bayley, St. †1821** • **Spiritual Conferences** • What was the first rule of our dear Savior's life? You know it was to do His Father's will. Well, then, the first end I propose in our daily work is to do the will of God. Secondly, do it in the manner He willed, and finally, do it because it is His will.

¶418 • **Leo XII, Pope †1829** • **Caritate Christi, No. 3 (1825)** • After showing the necessity of inner penance and preparing souls for its acquisition, teach them Penance as a Sacrament. Let them be admonished that it is as necessary for those who have fallen after Baptism, as Baptism is for those who have not yet received it. Therefore, it is appropriately called "a plank after shipwreck," with which alone it is possible to reach the port of eternal salvation.

Even when sins have been washed away by absolution and eternal punishment relaxed, temporal punishment often remains.

¶419 • **Pius VIII, Pope †1830** • **Traditi Humilitati, No. 8 (1829)** • From the seminaries must come men well instructed both in

Christian and Church discipline and in the principles of
sound doctrine. Such men may then distinguish themselves
for their piety and teaching. . . .

Be very careful in choosing seminarians, since the
salvation of the people principally depends on good pastors.
Nothing contributes more to the ruin of souls than impious,
weak, or uninformed clerics.

¶420 • Möhler, Johann Adam (1796 - 1838) • Symbolism, Ch. 39 •
This accordingly is the doctrine of Catholics. You will obtain
the full and entire knowledge of the Catholic religion only in
connection with its essential form, which is the Church.

Look at the Scripture in an ecclesiastical spirit and it will
present you an image perfectly resembling the Church.
Contemplate Christ in and with His creation — the Church,
the only adequate authority representing Him — and you
will then stamp His image on your soul.

¶421 • Gregory XVI, Pope †1846 • Probe Nostis, No. 6 (1840) • We
are thankful for the success of apostolic missions in America,
the Indies, and other lands without the Faith. The
indefatigable zeal of many apostolic men has led them abroad
into those places. Relying not on wealth nor on any army,
they are protected by the shield of faith alone. . . . They are
inspired with a burning love and undeterred by rough roads
and heavy toil.

¶422 • Gallitzin, Demetrius, Prince (1770 - 1840) • Letter (1836) •
Whatever differences on points of doctrine may exist among
the different denominations of Christians, *all* should be
united in the bonds of charity, *all* should pray for one
another, *all* should be willing to assist one another; and when
we are compelled to disapprove of our neighbor's doctrine, let
our disapprobation fall upon his doctrine, not upon his
person.

¶423 • **Chateaubriand, François René (1768 - 1848)** • **The Genius of Christianity, Ch. 8** • Religion alone can renew the original energy of a nation. That of Christ had already laid the moral foundation. . . .

Jesus Christ may therefore, with strict truth, be called, in a material sense, that Savior of the world which He is in the spiritual sense. His career on earth was, even humanly speaking, the most important event that ever occurred among men, since the regeneration of society commenced only with the proclamation of the Gospel.

¶424 • **John Mary Vianney, St. (Curé of Ars) †1859** • **Catechism** • My little children, your hearts are small, but prayer stretches them and makes them capable of loving God. Through prayer we receive a foretaste of heaven and something of paradise comes down upon us. Prayer never leaves us without sweetness. It is honey that flows into the soul and makes all things sweet. When we pray properly, sorrows disappear like the snow before the sun.

Prayer is nothing else but union with God.

¶425 • **Gabriel of the Sorrowful Mother, St. †1862** • **Prayer** • Help me, O my God, to conquer myself! This I ask through Your infinite mercy. To obtain it I offer You the merits of Jesus Christ, Our Savior and Lord. I have no merits of my own; I am destitute, but His wounds will be my plea. Had I shed my blood for love of You, like Your Son, would You grant me this favor? How much more should You hear me, since He shed His Blood for me?

¶426 • **Faber, Frederick William †1863** • **The Right Must Win** • For right is right, since God is God; / And right the day must win; / To doubt would be disloyalty, / To falter would be sin.

¶427 • **Hughes, John, Archbishop †1864** • **Letters** • The Catholic Church is not a party in the politics of any nation, at home or abroad. Her mission is to all nations, and to all parties in each, except as either may be divided from the other by the eternal principles of right and wrong. She can never give up her mission and her message to all for the sake of only some.

¶428 • **Madeleine Sophie Barat, St. †1865** • **On Prayer** • When the love of Jesus is in question, let your generosity know no bounds; we can never bear enough for the God who suffered so much for us.

Let us love the Heart of Jesus the more, since it is wonderful and forgotten by so many. And if we, favored as we are, give Him but half a heart, what do we deserve?

Love God, and if you cannot meditate, always say, "My God, I love You."

¶429 • **Tabb, John Bannister (1845 - 1909)** • **Father Damien** • O God, the cleanest offering / Of tainted earth below, / Unblushing, to Thy feet we bring, / "A leper white as snow!"

¶430 • **_____** • **Recognition** • When Christ went up to Calvary, / His crown upon His head, / Each tree unto its fellow tree / In awful silence said: / "Behold the Gardener is He / Of Eden and Gethsemane."

¶431 • **Wiseman, Nicholas Cardinal †1865** • **Lectures, 3** • We allow no authority but the word of God, written or unwritten: and maintain that the control so necessary over the latter exists in the depository, that is, in the Church of Christ, which has been appointed by God to take charge of and keep safe these doctrines committed to her from the beginning, to be taught at all times to all nations.

¶432 • **Vatican Council I (1870)** • **Sess. 3** • Faith is the
supernatural virtue by which, through the help of God and
through the assistance of His grace, we believe what He has
revealed to be true, not on account of the intrinsic truth
perceived by the light of natural reason, but because of the
authority of God himself, the Revealer, Who can neither
deceive nor be deceived.

¶433 • _____ • **Sess. 4, Pastor Aeternus, No. 4** • We teach and
define that it is a dogma divinely revealed: that the Roman
Pontiff, when he speaks *ex cathedra*, that is, when in the
discharge of the office of pastor and doctor of all Christians,
by virtue of his supreme apostolic authority, he defines a
doctrine regarding faith or morals to be held by the universal
Church, by the divine assistance promised him in Blessed
Peter, is possessed of that infallibility with which the Divine
Redeemer willed that His Church should be endowed for
defining doctrine regarding faith or morals: and that
therefore such definitions of the Roman Pontiff are
irreformable of themselves, and not from the consent of the
Church.

¶434 • **Ullathorne, William Bernard, Archbishop
(1806-1889)** • **Humility and Patience (c. 1870)** • Beware of anxiety.
Next to sin there is nothing that troubles the mind so much,
strains the heart, distresses the soul, and confuses
judgment. . . . There is but one remedy for anxiety, and that
is by using the firm voice of patience to keep the objects of
our solicitude in their proper place.

¶435 • **Anthony Mary Claret, St. †1870** • **Correspondence** •
Because he is also concerned for his neighbor, the man of zeal
works to fulfill his desire that all be content on this earth and
happy and blessed in their heavenly homeland, that all may
be saved, and that no one perish forever, or offend God, or
remain even for a moment in sin.

Such are the concerns we observe in the holy apostles, and in all who are driven by the apostolic spirit.

¶436 • **Guéranger, Prosper (1805 - 1875)** • **The Liturgical Year, Ch. 1** • With regard to our Savior's birth on Dec. 25, we have St. John Chrysostom telling us, in his homily for this feast, that the Western Churches had, from the very commencement of Christianity, kept it on this day. He is not satisfied with merely mentioning the tradition; he undertakes to show that it is well-founded, inasmuch as the Church of Rome had every means of knowing the true day of our Savior's birth since the acts of enrollment, taken in Judea, were kept in the public archives of Rome.

The holy doctor adds a second argument which he founds on the Gospel of St. Luke, and he reasons thus: we know from the Sacred Scripture that it must have been in the fast in the seventh month that the priest Zachary had the vision in the Temple; after which Elizabeth his wife conceived St. John the Baptizer; hence it follows that the Blessed Virgin Mary having, as the evangelist St. Luke relates, received the Angel Gabriel's visit and conceived the Savior of the world in the sixth month of Elizabeth's pregnancy, that is to say, in March, the birth of Jesus must have taken place in the month of December.

¶437 • **Brownson, Orestes Augustus (1803 - 1876)** • **The American Republic, Ch. 14** • The infusion of the Christian dogma of the unity and solidarity of the human race into the belief, the life, the laws, the jurisprudence of all civilized nations, has doomed slavery and every species of barbarism.

¶438 • _____ • **The Convert** • There is little use in arguing the objections of non-Catholics, or in laboring directly for their refutation. We can effectually remove them only by correcting the premises from which the unbeliever reasons, and giving him first principles, which really enlighten his

reason, and, as they become operative, expel his error by
their own light and force.

¶439 • **Pius IX, Pope †1878** • **Graves ac Diuturnae, No. 7** • You
know very well how precious is the gift of your Catholic faith
which God has bestowed upon you. Never spare any care,
any effort to preserve that gift faithfully. Preserve safe and
sound the glory of that ancient faith which you received from
your ancestors.

¶440 • _____ • **Qui Pluribus, No. 10** • God himself has set
up a living authority to establish and teach the true and
legitimate meaning of His heavenly revelation. The authority
judges infallibly all disputes which concern matters of faith
and morals, lest the faithful be swirled around by every wind
of doctrine which springs from the evilness of man in
encompassing error.

¶441 • **Spalding, John Lancaster, Bishop (1840-1916)** • **Ave Maria
Bells, v. 1** • At dawn the joyful choir of bells, / In consecrated
citadels, / Flings on the sweet and drowsy air / A brief,
melodious call to prayer; / For Mary, Virgin meek and
lowly / Conceived of the Spirit Holy, / As the Lord's angel
did declare.

¶442 • **Digby, Kenelm †1880** • **Erin** • For grandeur, nations,
kingdoms have their day, / But faith like thine will never
pass away.

¶443 • **Ward, William G. †1882** • **Saying** • I should like a new
papal bull served every morning with my *Times* at breakfast.

¶444 • **Hecker, Isaac (1818 - 1888)** • **The Church and the Age** • If
there be any superior merit in the republican polity of the
United States, it consists chiefly in this: that while it adds
nothing and can add nothing to man's natural rights, it

expresses them more clearly, guards them more securely, and protects them more effectively; so that man, under its popular institutions, enjoys greater liberty in working out his true destiny.

¶445 • **John Bosco, St. †1888** • **Letter to His Companions** • This was the method that Christ used with the apostles. He put up with their ignorance and roughness and even their infidelity. He treated sinners with kindness and affection so that He caused some to be shocked, others to be scandalized, and still others to hope for God's mercy. And so He commanded us to be gentle and humble of heart.

¶446 • **Scheeben, Matthias J. (1835 - 1888)** • **The Mysteries of Christianity, 12:50** • The God-Man is an absolutely supernatural mystery for two reasons: first, because His human nature is not joined to another created essence, but is elevated above all the boundaries of the created world and united to the divine substance far more closely than it could be through grace; and secondly, because this kind of union is not a union in nature, nor is it a union such as could be found in the sphere of created nature at all, but is an absolutely unique, supereminent union.

¶447 • _____ • **The Mysteries of Christianity, 19:78** • What high, supernatural dignity is attained by man when he becomes a member of the Church, how astounding the union into which he enters with Christ, and through Christ with God, and at the same time with all his fellow members in the Church!

What a tremendous mystery lies even in simple membership in the Church! It is a mystery as great as the mystery of the mystical Body of Christ, as the mystery of the Eucharist in which it culminates, as the mystery of the Incarnation upon which it is based, as the mystery of grace which is its fruit.

¶448 • **Hopkins, Gerard Manley, S.J. †1889** • **Pied Beauty** • Glory be to God for dappled things — / For skies of couple-colour as a brindled cow; / For rose-moles all in stipple upon trout that swim; / Fresh-firecoal chestnut-falls; finches' wings; / Landscape plotted and pierced — fold, fallow, and plough; / And áll trádes, their gear and tackle trim. / All things counter, original, spare, strange; / Whatever is fickle, freckled (who knows how?) / With swift, slow; sweet, sour; adazzle, dim; / He fathers-forth whose beauty is past change; / Praise Him!

¶449 • **Newman, John Henry, Cardinal (1801 - 1890)** • **Apologia pro Vita Sua** • In spite of my ingrained fears of Rome, and the decision of my reason and conscience against her usages, in spite of my affection for Oxford and Oriel, yet I had a secret longing love of Rome, the mother of English Christianity, and I had a true devotion to the Blessed Virgin, in whose college I lived, whose altar I served, and whose immaculate purity I had in one of my earliest sermons made much of. . . .

When I was fully confident that the Church of Rome was the only, true Church, I joined her.

¶450 • _____ • **The Idea of a University, 8:10** • It is almost a definition of a gentleman to say that he is one who never inflicts pain. This description is both refined and, as far as it goes, accurate. The true gentleman in like manner carefully avoids whatever may cause a jar or a jolt in the minds of those with whom he is cast. . . . He makes light of favours while he does them, and seems to be receiving when he is conferring. He never speaks of himself except when compelled to. . . .

Such are some of the lineament of the ethical character which the cultivated intellect will form, apart from religious principle.

¶451 • _____ • **On the Inspiration of Scripture** • As to the

authority of Scripture, we hold it to be, in all matters of faith
and morals, divinely inspired throughout; as to its
interpretation, we hold that the Church is, in faith and
morals, the one infallible expounder of that inspired text.

¶452 • _____ • **Tracts for the Times, No. 87** • The Bible. . . .
Its light is like the body of heaven in its clearness; its
vastness like the bosom of the sea; its variety like scenes of
nature.

¶453 • **Manning, Henry, Cardinal †1892** • **The Eternal Priesthood** •
The divine office is a part of the divine tradition. It is a
perpetual witness for God and for the Faith. It has been
wrought together by the hands of men, but these men were
saints . . . and the materials of which it is composed are the
words of the Spirit of God. . . . The psalms and scriptures of
inspired men under the old law and the new, with the
writings of the saints, are all interwoven into a wonderful
texture of prayer and praise, of worship and witness of the
kingdom of God and of the communion of saints.

¶454 • **McQuaid, Bernard, Bishop †1909** • **Address, Nov. 25, 1894** •
It has been traditional in the Church in the United States for
bishops to hold aloof from politics. This tradition has been
handed down to us by bishops whose greatness was real, not
merely newspaper greatness. . . . Although often accused, by
our enemies, of actively participating in political plottings
and partisanship, we have been able to deny and repel the
false accusation.

¶455 • _____ • **Address to Religious Teachers, 1892** • The
purpose of your life in becoming Religious was that you
might concentrate all the faculties of your mind, your soul,
your body to the highest service of God possible for a woman.
You were not afraid to stand before God and make a sacrifice
of life in its fullness and completeness. A higher sacrifice

than yours I do not know, nor am I aware of one from which greater good is bound to come.

¶456 • **Ireland, John, Archbishop (c. 1838 - 1918)** • **The Church and Modern Society** • The mission of the Catholic Church to the world is the same as it has been for nineteen hundred years; but the world has changed and is changing. With the new order have come new needs, new hopes, new aspirations. To conquer the world for Christ, the Church must herself be new, adapting herself in manner of life and in method of action to the conditions of the new order, thus proving herself, while ever ancient, to be ever new, as truth from heaven is and even must be.

¶457 • _____ • **On American Citizenship** • I have called America the providential nation. Even as I believe that God rules over men and nations, so do I believe that a divine mission has been assigned to the Republic of the United States. That mission is to prepare the world, by example and moral influence, for the universal reign of human liberty and human rights. America does not live for herself alone; the destinies of humanity are in her keeping.

¶458 • **Pasteur, Louis †1895** • **Of his dying daughter. . .** • I know only scientifically determined truth, but I am going to believe what I wish to believe, what I cannot help but believe — I expect to meet this dear child in another world.

¶459 • **Patmore, Coventry †1896** • **Religio Poetae** • In recent times, genius and imagination have come to be widely regarded as one and the same thing. They are not so, however, though they are perhaps indissolubly connected. The most peculiar and characteristic mark of genius is insights into subjects which are dark to ordinary vision and for which ordinary language has no adequate expression.

Imagination is rather the language of genius: the power

which traverses at a single glance the whole external universe, and seizes on the likenesses and images, and their combinations, which are best able to embody ideas and feelings otherwise inexpressible; so that the things which are unseen are known by the things which are seen.

¶460 • Thérèse of the Child Jesus, St. (1873 - 1897) • Autobiography
• By chance I turned to the twelfth and thirteenth chapters of the First Letter to the Corinthians. I found this theme: "Set your desires on the greater gifts. And I will show you the way that surpasses all the others."

The Apostle insists that the greater gifts are nothing at all without love, and that this same love is surely the best path leading directly to God. At length, I had found peace of mind.

My call is love. In the heart of the Church, my Mother, I will be love.

¶461 • Johnson, Lionel †1902 • To My Patrons, vv. 4, 6 •
Remembering God's coronation day; / Thorns for His crown; His throne a cross: to thee / Heaven's kingdom dearer was than earth's. Then pray, / Saint Louis! to the King of kings for me.

Bishop of souls in servitude astray, / Who didst for holy service set them free: / Use still thy discipline of love, and pray, / Saint Charles! unto the world's High Priest for me.

¶462 • Acton, John Emmerich Dalberg Lord †1902 • Ultramontanism
• There are two things which it specially behooves every Catholic engaged in controversy to observe in his treatment of adversaries: that the discussion ought to be a means of converting them from error, instead of repelling them from the truth by the faults of its defenders; and that no bitterness or personality should scandalize them by occasions of sin.

¶463 • _____ • Power* (in Letter to Bishop Creighton, 1887) •
Power tends to corrupt; absolute power corrupts absolutely.

[*This saying, in various forms, has been attributed to several different authors.]

¶464 • **Leo XIII, Pope (1810 - 1903)** • **Rerum Novarum, Nos. 15, 26, 36** • Let it be regarded as established that in seeking help for the masses, this principle before all others is to be considered basic: that private ownership must be preserved inviolate. . . .

Private possessions are clearly in accord with nature. . . .

To own goods privately is a right natural to man, and to exercise this right, especially in life in society, is not only lawful but clearly necessary.

¶465 • _____ • **Tametsi Futura, No. 6** • In God alone can the human will find absolute and perfect peace. God is the only end of man. All our life on earth is the truthful and exact image of a pilgrimage.

Now, Christ is the Way, for we can never reach God, the supreme and ultimate Good, by this toilsome and doubtful road of mortal life, except with Christ as our leader and guide.

How so? First and chiefly by His grace; but this would remain "void" in man if the precepts of His law were neglected.

¶466 • **Gemma Galgani, St. †1903** • **Prayer** • Assist me, my Jesus, for I desire to become good whatsoever it may cost; take away, destroy, utterly root out all that You find in me contrary to Your holy will. At the same time, I pray You, Lord Jesus, to enlighten me that I may be able to walk in Your holy light. Amen.

[8]
Twentieth Century: Triumphant

The twentieth century burst into history with notable optimism and a sense of triumphalism. King Edward VII was crowned in London; the United States took over Cuba as a protectorate; the Boxer Uprising was settled in China; Teddy Roosevelt took over the presidency of the United States and signed a treaty to build the Panama Canal. It was all very positive.

As the new century proceeded, the enthusiasm was little dampened by the Russo-Japanese war, the foundation of the I.W.W., and the formation of the Union of South Africa on the basis of apartheid. Sun Yat Sen was active in China in a movement that would make that country democratic.

Even as tensions built up among the Great Powers, no one really expected the First World War, or its length and intensity. The Peace Treaty of Versailles left Germany a "basket case," and ripe for the dreams of a young fanatic named Adolf Hitler.

After the heady, swinging 1920s, the Black Friday on the New York Stock Market on Wall Street in 1929 heralded one of the worst economic depressions known to history. As the 1930s progressed, things just became worse and worse. Franklin Roosevelt, the fabled FDR, promised America a "New Deal" and led the country to a partial recovery.

But events in Europe and the Far East brought on World War II, which involved even more cruelty and intensity. It had been preceded by "The Holocaust," during which Hitler tried genocide, the extermination of the Jewish race.

With these two clouds darkening the twentieth century, could there be worse? The United Nations Organization, begun with even more dreams than the League of Nations, became nothing more than a usually polite and boring debating society.

The Cold War developed between Russia and her satellites and the Western Powers. Churchill spoke of the Iron Curtain that had descended on Europe. Add to this the Korean War and the Vietnam War and people everywhere wondered how this century would end.

Even the bright hopes brought on by the tragically short presidency of John F. Kennedy, JFK, were to be dashed.

And how did the Church respond and react throughout this period? It, too, enjoyed an era of triumphalism, probably unparalleled since the early fourteenth century. Heady with the aftermath of the definition of papal infallibility, it seemed as if the Vatican could rule supreme and serene.

Fortunately for the Church, the modern popes, since Leo XIII, were men of great ability and leadership. They reacted very well to the currents of history around them.

Leo XIII and Pius XI fought bravely for the rights of the working man. Benedict XV worked mightily for peace during World War I. Pope St. Pius X gave Holy Communion back to the children, and urged frequent Communion for everyone. Pope Pius XII seemed to be involved in everything, after Pius XI had solved the Italian Question with the Vatican Concordat with Italy.

Except for the years around 1931-34, the Church responded to the material needs of the poor with great generosity, and the American Church will go down in history for the magnitude of its donations to the needy all over the world. The American bishops founded the National Catholic Welfare Organization, which was later succeeded by the Catholic Relief Services, the largest private charitable organization in the world, ever. Some outstanding individuals like Dom Lukas Etlin, O.S.B., worked for the seminaries and dioceses in war-torn Europe.

There were interesting theological growth and reflection,

and literary giants like Chesterton and Belloc. And throughout the first half of the twentieth century, there were voices that raised questions about the spiritual depth that was uncertain beneath the note of triumphalism. Without knowing it, they were pointing to Vatican II.

¶467 • **Wilde, Oscar †1900** • **The Ballad of Reading Gaol, 5** • This too I know — and wise it were / If each could know the same — / That every prison that men build / Is built with bricks of shame, / And bound with bars, lest Christ should see / How men their brothers maim.

¶468 • **De Vere, Aubrey †1902** • **Corpus Christi** • Rejoice! ye angels, and thou Church, / This day triumphant here below; / He comes in meekest emblems clad, / Himself He cometh to bestow. / That Body which thou gavest, O earth, / He giveth back — that Flesh, that Blood, / Born of the altar's mystic birth, / At once thy worship and thy food.

¶469 • **Walsh, James J. (1865-1942)** • **Thirteenth: The Greatest of Centuries (1907), p. 21** • The universities were a natural growth from the favoring soil in which living seeds were planted. They sprang from the wonderful inquiring spirit of the time and the marvelous desire for knowledge and for the higher intellectual life that came over the people of Europe during the Thirteenth Century. . . .

Nearly all of the features of university life during the Thirteenth Century emphasize the democracy of feeling of the students, and make it clear that the blowing of the wind and the spirit of human liberty and intellectual enthusiasm influencing the minds of the generation is the underlying feature of university foundation and development.

¶470 • _____ • **Thirteenth: The Greatest of Centuries, p. 249** • These mystery and morality plays of the Thirteenth Century brought the people intimately into contact with the great characters of the Old Testament and the New Testament, and besides giving them precise religious information helped them to an insight into character and to a right appreciation of human actions, and a sympathy with what was right even though it entailed suffering, such as could not otherwise have been obtained.

¶471 •**Vagaggini, Cipriano (1909-). • Theological Dimensions, Ch. 2 •** It is characteristic of the liturgy to be an action, a communitarian action of the assembly in which the members all have a role to play, an action centered on the Mass and the sacraments, finally an action whose whole meaning is to have the mystery of Christ relived by those who take part in it.

¶472 • **Pius X, Pope St. †1914 • Editae Saepa, No. 4 •** We are of the opinion that the shining example of Christ's soldiers has far greater value in the winning and sanctifying of souls than the words of profound treatises. We gladly take this opportunity to teach some very useful lessons from the consideration of the life of another holy pastor whom God raised up in the midst of trials very similar to those we are experiencing today.

We refer to St. Charles Borromeo, Cardinal of the Holy Roman Church and Archbishop of Milan, whom Paul V of holy memory raised to the altar of the saints less than thirty years after his death.

¶473 • _____ • **Il Fermo Proposito, No. 9 •** The Church, in her long history and on every occasion, has wisely shown that she possesses the marvelous power of adapting herself to the changing conditions of civil society. Thus, while preserving the integrity and immutability of faith and morals and upholding her sacred rights, she easily bends and accommodates herself to all the unessential and accidental circumstance belonging to various stages of civilization and to the new requirements of civil society.

¶474 • Thompson, Francis (1859 - 1907) • The Hound of Heaven (beginning) • I fled Him, down the nights and down the days; / I fled Him, down the arches of the years; / I fled Him, down the labyrinthine ways / Of my own mind; and in the midst of tears / I hid from Him, and under running laughter. / Up vistaed hopes I sped; / And shot, precipitated, / Adown Titanic glooms of chasmed fears, / From those strong feet that followed, followed after. . . .

¶475 • Benson, Robert Hugh †1914 • After a Retreat, v. 1 • What hast thou learned today? / Hast thou sounded awful mysteries, / Hast pierced the veiled skies, / Climbed to the feet of God, / Trodden where the saints have trod, / Fathomed the heights above? / *May: This only have I learned, that God is love.*

¶476 • _____ • Christ in the Church • Divine truth must always be extreme: it must, so to speak, always overlap at both ends, just because it is divine, and therefore much too big for this world. . . .

Religion must at least touch the will: for however small our will may be, it is always large enough to be united with the will of God.

¶477 • Benedict XV, Pope †1922 • Ad Beatissimi Apostolorum, No. 24 • Such is the nature of Catholicism that it does not admit of more or less, but must be held as a whole, or as a whole rejected. "This is the Catholic Faith, which unless a man believes faithfully and firmly, he cannot be saved" (Athanasian Creed).

There is no need of adding any qualifying terms to the profession of Catholicism: it is quite enough for each one to proclaim: "Christian is my name and Catholic my surname," only let him endeavor to be in reality what he calls himself.

¶478 • **Kilmer, (Alfred) Joyce** †1918 • **Trees** • I think that I shall never see / A poem lovely as a tree; / A tree whose hungry mouth is prest / Against the earth's sweet flowing breast; / A tree that looks at God all day, / And lifts her leafy arms to pray; / A tree that may in summer wear / A nest of robins in her hair; / Upon whose bosom snow has lain, / Who intimately lives with rain. / Poems are made by fools like me, / But only God can make a tree.

¶479 • **Charles de Foucauld** †1916 • **Letter (1915)** • To be an apostle, but how? / With goodness and kindness, brotherly affection, a virtuous example, with humility and tenderness which are always impressive and Christian. . . .

To some, without ever saying to them anything about God or religion, being patient as God is patient, being good as God is good, being a kind brother and praying. . . .

To others, speaking of God as much as they are able to take. Above all, to see a brother in every human being, to see in every human being a son of God, a person redeemed by the blood of Jesus.

¶480 • _____ • **Letters (1916)** • God makes me find in the solitude and silence a consolation on which I had not counted. I am constantly, absolutely constantly, with Him and with those I love. . . .

I see all things in the light of the immense peace of God, of His infinite happiness, of the immutable glory of the blessed and ever-tranquil Trinity. Everything loses itself for me in the happiness that God is God.

¶481 • _____ • **Prayer*** • I cannot conceive of love that feels no constraining need of resembling, of becoming like

You, and especially sharing all the hurts and pains, all the difficulties, all the hardships of life. . . .

I judge no one, Lord, for the others are also Your servants, and my brothers, and I must love them.

But it is impossible for me, myself, to understand how one can love You and not seek to resemble You, and not feel the need of sharing every cross.

[*Quoted by René Voillaume in *Seeds of the Desert*, Ch. 5.]

¶482 • **Ward, Wilfrid** †1916 • **Witnesses to the Unseen** • As St. Philip Neri, by his love for those who leant upon him, and by his personal character, drew all men to him for guidance and advice, winning respect and esteem from Jews and infidels as well as members of the Church, so did Newman by the power of his personality find himself the center of influence among vast numbers of priests and laymen, non-Catholics as well as Catholics.

The simple priest was by popular voice called the apostle of Rome; the English Oratorian was, as a representative critic has expressed it, "canonized" by the voice of the English people.

¶483 • **Plunkett, Joseph Mary** †1916 • **I See His Blood Upon the Rose** • I see His Blood upon the rose / And in the stars the glory of His eyes, / His Body gleams amid the eternal skies.

I see His face in every flower; / The thunder and the singing of the birds / Are but His voice — and carven by His power, / Rocks are His written words.

All pathways by His feet are worn, / His strong Heart stirs the ever-beating sea, / His Crown of Thorns is twined with every thorn, / His cross is every tree.

¶484 • **Frances Xavier Cabrini, St.** †1917 • **Prayer** • Fortify me with the grace of Your Holy Spirit and give Your peace to my soul that I may be free from all needless anxiety, solicitude, and worry. Help me to desire always that which is pleasing and acceptable to You so that Your will may be my will.

¶485 • **U.S. Bishops** • **Pastoral Letter, 1919** • In our own country there are fields of missionary labor that call in a special manner for assiduous cultivation. There are races less fortunate in a worldly sense, and, for that very reason, more fully dependent on Christian zeal.

The lot of the Negro and the Indian, though latterly much improved, is far from being what the Church would desire. Both have been hampered by adverse conditions. . . . In the eyes of the Church there is no distinction of race or nation; there are human souls, and these have all alike been purchased at the same great price, the Blood of Jesus Christ.

¶486 • _____ • **Pastoral Letter, 1919 (concl.)** • The fact that men are striving for what they consider to be their rights, puts their dispute on a moral basis; and, wherever justice may lie, whichever of the opposing claims may have the better foundation, it is justice that all demand.

¶487 • **Gibbons, Cardinal James (1834 - 1921)** • **Faith of Our Fathers, Ch. 8** • The Church is the only divinely constituted teacher of Revelation.

Now, the Scripture is the great depository of the Word of God. Therefore, the Church is the divinely appointed Custodian and Interpreter of the Bible. Indeed, her infallible Guide would be superfluous if each individual could interpret the Bible for himself.

¶488 • **Marmion, Dom Joseph Columba, Abbot (1858 - 1923)** • **Christ in His Mysteries, Ch. 7** • We ask to be partakers of that divinity to which our human nature is united. It is like an exchange. God, in becoming Incarnate, takes our human nature and gives us, in return, a participation in His Divine Nature.

O admirabile commercium! "O Admirable Exchange! The

Creator of the human race, taking upon Himself a body and a soul, has vouchsafed to be born of a Virgin, and, appearing here below as man, has made us partakers of His divinity" (Antiphon, Octave of Christmas).

¶489 • _____ • **Christ the Ideal of the Monk, Preface** • Christ Jesus is the sublime Ideal of all holiness, the Divine Model presented by God himself to the imitation of His elect. Christian holiness consists in the complete and sincere acceptance of Christ by faith, and in the expansion of this faith by hope and charity; it implies the stable and total hold exercised by Christ upon our activity through the supernatural influence of His Spirit.

Christ Jesus, the Alpha and Omega of all our works, becomes by the communication of His own life, the very life of our souls: "For me to live is Christ."

¶490 • _____ • **Christ the Ideal of the Priest, Ch. 16, No. 1** • According to the designs of the Father, it is by faith that the children of adoption must enter into contact with the supernatural world: with Christ, the Church, the sacraments and above all, the Eucharist. It is by faith that they must hope in God, love Him, and serve Him.

¶491 • _____ • **Christ the Life of the Soul, Ch. 1, No. 1** • All holiness is to consist in this: to receive the divine life from Christ and by Christ, who possesses its fullness and who has been constituted the one Mediator; to keep this divine life and increase in it unceasingly by an ever more perfect adherence, an ever closer union with Him who is its source.

Holiness is a mystery of divine life communicated and received, communicated to humanity by the Son, so that Christ is truly the life of the soul because He is the source and giver of life.

¶492 • _____ • **Fire of Love, Ch. 14** • The gifts of the divine Spirit perfect the virtues by disposing us to act with a supernatural assurance which constitutes in us what is like a divine instinct of heavenly things. By these gifts, which the Holy Spirit places within us to render us more docile to His action, He achieves the work of making us more and more the children of God. "For whoever are led by the Spirit of God, they are the sons of God" (Gal. 5:22-23).

¶493 • **Lunn, Sir Arnold (1888 - 1974)** • **Now I See (c. 1925)** • It is significant that freedom of speech and action has never been more ruthlessly suppressed than in the one great European nation which has officially adopted atheism as the religion of the state.

¶494 • **Hawthorne-Lathrop, Rose (Mother Alphonsa, 1851-1926)** • **A Protean Glimpse** • Time, the messenger of fate! / Cunning master of debate, / Cunning soother of all sorrow, / Ruthless robber of tomorrow, / Tyrant of our dallying feet, / Though patron of a life complete.

¶495 • **Gasquet, Francis Neil Aidan, Cardinal †1929** • **Parish Life in England Before the Reformation** • The parish wardens had their duties towards the poorer members of the district. In more than one instance they were the guardians of the common chest, out of which temporary loans could be obtained by needy parishioners, to tide over persons in difficulties. These loans were secured by pledges and the additional security of other parishioners. No interest was charged for the use of the money.

¶496 • **Bolton, Herbert (1870 - 1953** • **Rim of Christendom, (c. 1930)** p. 4 • The Black Robes [Jesuits] of New France counted their conversions by the hundreds, or at best by the thousands. Those of New Spain, working in a more propitious vineyard, numbered their baptisms by the hundreds of thousands, or even by the millions.

The imposing stature of the Jesuits in New France is widely known. The Spanish Jesuits in North America still await their historian.

¶497 • **Coughlin, Charles E. (1891 - 1979)** • **Without Religion, What?** **(1931), Concl.** • Behold the star of the East! Its silvery gleam once led the Wise Men across the deserts and through the night ot the humble, despised crib at Bethlehem. The same star scintillates on high today! The same Prince of Peace is there to welcome you as He once welcomed the humble shepherds. "Come to Me all ye who labor and are heavily burdened and I will refresh you."

¶498 • _____ • **Gold and Silver** • The policies of greed must give way to gestures of Christianity. We shall not participate in any national or international action whose main object and motive is to cut in half the values, the livelihood, the food, the clothing of sixty-five per cent of the population of this world. By doing so, we not only become cooperators in one of the most dastardly crimes of history by thus inflicting pain upon foreign nations. We also become treacherous betrayers of our own citizens whose livelihood is so much dependent on the purchasing power of foreign buyers.

¶499 • **Chapman, John, Abbot †1933** • **Bishop Gore and the Catholic Claims** • The Catholic Church cannot insist too much on the true position of Mary, for it is a strong hedge around the doctrine of the Incarnation. Every grace of Mary's, every prerogative, every dignity she has, is hers simply because she is the Mother of God; and it is only for the sake of Christ that we honor her, nor do we give her any honor which does not in consequence redound to Him of necessity.

¶500 • **Chesterton, Gilbert Keith †1936** • **Benedicamus Domino** • Wherever a Catholic sun doth shine, / There's plenty of laughter and good red wine. / God grant that it be ever so, / Benedicamus Domino.

¶501 • _____ • **The Defendant** • The Iliad is only great because all life is a battle; the Odyssey, because all life is a journey; the Book of Job, because all life is a riddle.

¶502 • _____ • **The Everlasting Man, Ch 2, No. 2** • We have all heard people say a hundred times over that the Jesus of the New Testament is indeed a most merciful and humane lover of humanity, but the Church has hidden this human characteristic in repellent dogmas and stiffened it with ecclesiastical terrors till it has taken on an inhuman character.

That is, I venture to repeat, very nearly the reverse of the truth. The truth is that it is the image of Christ in the Churches that is almost entirely mild and merciful. It is the image of Christ in the Gospels that is a good many other things as well.

¶503 • **Lagrange, Marie Joseph (1855 - 1938)** • **The Gospel of Jesus Christ, Ch. 7** • Pious children of the Church entertain no doubt that the newly risen Savior appeared first of all to His most holy Mother. She had fed Him at her breast, she had guided Him in His childhood years, she had, so to say, introduced Him to the world at the marriage feast of Cana, and beyond that she hardly appears again in the Gospel until she stands at the foot of the cross.

But to her alone, with Joseph, Jesus had devoted the thirty years of His hidden life, and would He not have reserved for her alone also the first moments of His new life that was hidden in God?

¶504 • **Goodier, Alban, Archbishop** †1939 • **The Inner Life of the Catholic** • The strength of the Church in her unity, which nothing is able to break, not because it is too strong, for humanly it is weak, but because it is a unity that is not of this earth.

¶505 • **Pius XI, Pope** †1939 • **Divini Redemptoris, No. 10** • Communism strips man of his liberty, robs human personality of all its dignity, and removes all the moral restraints that check the eruptions of blind impulse. There is no recognition of any right of the individual in his relations to the collectivity; no natural right is accorded to human personality, which is a mere cogwheel in the Communist system.

¶506 • _____ • **Quadragesimo Anno, Nos. 45, 46** • Nature, rather the Creator himself, has given man the right of private ownership not only that individuals may be able to provide for themselves and their families, but also that the good which the Creator destined for the entire family of mankind may through this institution truly serve this purpose.

Accordingly, twin rocks of shipwreck must be carefully avoided. For, as one is wrecked upon what is known as "individualism" by denying or minimizing the social and public character of the right of property, so by rejecting or minimizing the private and individual character of this same right, one inevitably runs into "collectivism" or at least closely approaches its tenets.

¶507 • **Quirk, Charles, S.J. (1889 - 1962)** • **The Countersign (c. 1940)** • An erstwhile sinner knocked at heaven's gate, / Without the password dread. / "I know no countersign, save sorrow, Lord." / "Pass in," our Savior said.

¶508 • **Mersch, Emile, S.J.** †1940 • **The Theology of the Mystical Body, Ch. 16, No. 1** • In the ordinary language of the Church, "mystical body" connotes the entire multitude of those who live the life of Christ, with a life that admits of degrees, whereas the word "Church" represents the society of the baptized faithful as organized under their lawful pastors.

¶509 • _____ • **The Whole Christ, Ch. 11, No. 5** • Each Christian has his own personal grace; yet in all who possess grace, all those individual graces remain united in their common source, which is Christ, the Head of the Church. In the supernatural order, there is but one living organism in Christ.

The organism grows and develops through the ages and it extends itself to all peoples over the entire face of the earth; yet all of this, all this life, all the good that is wrought in heaven by the saints and by men here on earth, in the whole universe, and throughout all time — all this is one Christ, Head and members.

¶510 • **Feeney, Leonard, S.J. †1978** • **Fish on Friday (c. 1940)** • For if one is Catholic, one cannot think without being cosmical, or without being comical, either, because the Faith links all realities together and fills the world with surprises.

¶511 • **Farrell, Walter, O.P. (1902 - 1951)** • **Companion to the Summa, v. 1, Ch.2 (1938-1942)** • Because nothing that is moved moves or changes itself, the unquestionable fact of movement or change in the world about us forces us to conclude to the existence of a first mover who is himself not moved.

We find that nothing that is, is the cause of itself Precisely because of this impossibility of a cause causing itself, the efficient causes of the sensible world force the conclusion on us that a first efficient cause exists which is itself uncaused.

¶512 • **Lynch, John W. (1904-)** • **A Woman Wrapped in Silence, Ch. 11 (1941)** • Luke of course has written down / What he had

heard as once before in like / Simplicity he wrote of
swaddling bands, / And only that she brought Him forth and
laid / Him, crying, in a manger, and He . . . / Not written
what He might have seen beneath / her eyes that dreamed so
deep of more than dreams. / There is so much of Him that is
her own. . . .

¶513 • **Maximilian Kolbe, St. †1941** • **First Editorial** • Everyone
cannot become a genius, but the path of holiness is open to
all. . . . It is untrue that the saints were not like us. They too
experienced temptations, they fell and rose again; they
experienced sorrow that weakened and paralyzed them with
a sense of discouragement. . . . They did not trust themselves
but placed all their trust in God.

¶514 • **Maynard, Theodore (1890 - 1956)** • **The Story of American
Catholicism, p. 26 (1941)** • We know what happened to Juan de
Padilla, the proto-martyr of America . . . [in what is now]
southwestern Kansas. They saw coming toward them a band
of hostile braves. . . . When Padilla had almost reached those
running towards him, he knelt down to meet death.

After the savages had done their bloody work, the two
Indian converts returned. Padilla's body was riddled with
arrows. They buried him with Christian prayers. It was from
them that we have the details of what happened.

We might note that this first martyrdom was not on the
coast but almost in the center of the continent. By it, the
whole of America was consecrated to Christ. (The year was
1541.)

¶515 • **Stein, Edith (Sister Teresa Benedicta a Cruce, O.Carm.)
†1942** • **Letter on the Carmelite Life (1933)** • My impression was that
this was a life which had been absolutely transformed by
God, down to the last detail. I simply can't imagine anything
greater. I would like to see this attitude incorporated as much

as possible into my own life and the lives of those who are dear to me.

¶516 • O'Connell, William, Cardinal †1944 • Letter on Workers' Rights • Capital has a right to a just share of the profits, but only a just share. . . .

Anyone who possesses a natural right may make use of all legitimate means to protect it, and to safeguard it from violation. . . .

The worker has the right to refuse to work, that is, to strike, and to induce by peaceful and lawful methods others to strike with him.

¶517 • Ryan, John Augustine (1869 - 1945) • Distributive Justice, Ch. 23 • Just as the woman worker who lives with her parents has a right to a wage sufficient to maintain her away from home, so the unmarried adult has the right to a family living wage.

If only married men get the latter wage, they will be discriminated against in the matter of employment. To prevent this obviously undesirable condition, it is necessary that a family living wage be recognized as the right of all adult workers. In a competitive regime, the standard wage for both the married and the unmarried is necessarily the same.

No other arrangement is reasonable in our present industrial system.

¶518 • Furfey, Paul Hanley (1896-) • The Respectable Murderers, Ch. 7 (c. 1950) • Possibly the chief obstacle to the understanding of Christian charity is its seeming simplicity. To say that man's supreme duty is to love God and his neighbor may sound too pat to be convincing.

Yet, the reality is not obvious; not the greatest contemplative saints could boast of understanding it fully. To obtain even an elementary insight into the nature of Christian love requires long and intense consideration.

¶519 • **Powers, Jessica (Sister Miriam of the Holy Spirit, O.C.D., 1907-) • Boundaries, c. 1950** • The heart can set its boundaries / On mortal acres without fear. / Descent of skies, cascade of seas / Are not to be expected here.

The heart can take a human love / To feed and shelter, if it will, / Nor think to see its cities move / In avalanches down a hill.

Only when God is passing by / And is invited in to stay / Is there a split of earth and sky. / Boundaries leap and rush away.

And wound and chaos come to be / Where once a world lay still and small, / But how else could Infinity / Enter what is dimensional?

¶520 • **Dawson, Christopher †1970 • Medieval Essays (c. 1950)** • The Middle Ages were not the ages of faith in the sense of unquestioning submission to the authority or to blind obedience. They were ages of spiritual struggle and social change, in which the existing situation was continually modified by the reforming energy and the intellectual activity that were generated by the contact between the living stream of Christian tradition and the youthful peoples of the West.

¶521 • **Davis, Henry, S.J. (1866 - 1952) • Moral and Pastoral Theology, Vol. 1, Ch. 6** • Conscience that is certain, that is, where its possessor is clearly convinced that his conscience unhesitatingly imposes a definite obligation here and now, in the concrete, must be obeyed. . . .

Conscience is an act of practical reason. It tells us that an action which appears to us to be morally bad must be omitted, that an action which is here and now commanded must, if possible, be performed.

¶522 • **Belloc, Hilaire †1953 • Courtesy, vv. 1-3** • Of courtesy, it is much less / Than courage of heart or holiness, / Yet in my walks it seems to me / That the Grace of God is in courtesy.

On monks I did in Storrington fall, / They took me straight into their hall; / I saw three pictures on a wall, / And Courtesy was in them all.

The first the Annunciation; / The second the Visitation; / The third, the Consolation / Of God that was Our Lady's Son.

¶523 • _____ • **The Great Heresies** • Now the most difficult thing in the world in connection with history, and the rarest of achievement, is the seeing of events as contemporaries saw them, instead of seeing them through the distorting medium of later knowledge.

¶524 • **Houselander, Caryll †1954** • **Guilt** • The prayers of the Church are the age-long poetry of mankind, lifted above the perfection of poetry, for they are the prayer of Christ on earth. This is what ritual means, with its ordered movements, its wide encircling gesture of love, its kiss of peace, its extended arms of sacrifice.

¶525 • **Teilhard de Chardin, Pierre, S.J. (1881 - 1955)** • **The Divine Milieu, 3:2** • To adore — That means to lose oneself in the unfathomable, to plunge into the inexhaustible, to find peace in the incorruptible, to be absorbed in defined immensity, to offer oneself, and to give of one's deepest to that whose depth has no end. Whom, then, can we adore?

O Jesus, show Yourself to us as the Mighty, the Radiant, the Risen!

¶526 • _____ • **The Divine Milieu, p. 106** • Christianity alone saves the essential aspiration of all mysticism: to be united (that is, to become the other) while remaining oneself. . . . We can only lose ourselves in God by prolonging the most individual characteristics of beings far beyond themselves;

that is the fundamental rule by which we can always
distinguish the true mystic from his counterfeits.

¶527 • **Drexel, Mother Katharine, S.B.S. †1955 • Reflections on Life
on the Vine, p. 7•** Jarring discord is the mark of enemies. Peace
and concord are the privilege of those who are on His side.
What did Our Lord do? He was silent. Jesus' silence teaches
us fortitude and humility; overeagerness to justify causes us
to commit faults. If I am silent, reverent, and humble, God
not only speaks for me, but to me in prayer.

The silence of Jesus is powerful.

¶528 • **_____ • Reflections on Life on the Vine, p. 10 •** The
Eucharist is the continuation of the Incarnation. In it Jesus
communicates himself to me and to every human heart and
becomes in very truth the Vine that bears God's plants,
sending the sap of His Divine Life into all their branches and
shoots, causing them to blossom and bear fruit into eternal
life.

¶529 • **Casey, Solanus, O.F.M. Cap. †1957 • Letters, 1937 •** Your
plan may prove to be sublime, if you'll await God's plan. We
cook up plans but turn ill with too much flavoring of self-will.
If this idea comes from heaven, be patient: it will grow like
leaven.

God descends to use our powers, if we don't spoil His plan
with ours. . . . We do God's work best when we obey, and
crucify self-will each day.

We seek God's glory, not our own. Then let us honor Him
alone. No matter if I preach or pray or sweep the floors or
mow the hay, the angels watch to recompense my loving,
prompt obedience.

¶530 • **Knox, Ronald A. †1957 • Stimuli •** The world has to be
saved by hook or by crook; it is well for the Church when
anglers and shepherds do not fall out.

¶531 • _____ • **Trials of a Translator: Farewell to Machabees** • Ecclesiastes and Wisdom are also philosophical arguments, though not in the form of a dialogue. The former is comparatively easy, but you have to watch your step all the time, or you find yourself missing the emphasis and therefore losing the thread.

Wisdom is so difficult that I toyed with the idea of writing a thesis to prove that it was written by St. Paul while still unconverted.

¶532 • **Pius XII, Pope †1958** • **Divino Afflante Spiritu, No. 28** • The Catholic exegete will find invaluable help in an assiduous study of those works in which the Holy Father, the Doctors of the Church, and the renowned interpreters of past ages have explained the Sacred Books.

For, although sometimes less instructed in profane learning and in the knowledge of languages than the scripture scholars of our time, nevertheless by reason of the office assigned to them by God in the Church, they are distinguished by a certain subtle insight into heavenly things and by a marvelous keenness of intellect, which enables them to penetrate to the very innermost meaning of the divine word and bring to light all that can help elucidate the teaching of Christ and promote holiness of life.

¶533 • _____ • **Doctor Mellifluus, No. 17** • Of this divine charity, possibly nobody has spoken more excellently, more profoundly, or more earnestly than Bernard: "The reason for loving God," he says, "is God; the measure of this love is to love without measure."

The "Doctor Mellifluus," the last of the Fathers, but certainly not inferior to the earlier ones, was remarkable for such qualities of nature and mind, and so enriched by God with heavenly gifts that, in the changing and often stormy times in which he lived, he seemed to dominate by his wisdom, holiness, and prudent counsel.

¶534 • _____ • **Mediator Dei, No. 40** • Only to the apostles, and thenceforth to those on whom their successors have imposed hands, is granted the power of the priesthood, in virtue of which they represent the person of Christ before their people, acting at the same time as representatives of their people before God. This priesthood is not transmitted by heredity or human descent.

It does not emanate from the Christian community. It is not a delegation from the people. Prior to acting as representative of the community before the throne of God, the priest is the ambassador of the divine Redeemer.

¶535 • _____ • **Meminisse Juvat, No. 5** • It is Christianity, above all others, which teaches the full truth, real justice, and that divine charity which drives away hatred, ill will, and enmity. Christianity has been given charge of these virtues by the Divine Redeemer who is the way, the truth, and the life, and she must do all in her power to put them to use.

Anyone, therefore, who knowingly ignores Christianity — the Catholic Church — or tries to hinder, demean or undo her, either weakens thereby the very basis of society, or tries to replace them with props not strong enough to support the edifice of human worth, freedom, and well-being.

¶536 • _____ • **Optatissima Pax, 1, 7** • Peace, longed for so hopefully, which should signify the tranquillity of order and serene liberty, even after the cruel experience of a long war, still hangs in an uncertain balance, as everyone must note with sadness and alarm.

It must be clearly understood and constantly borne in mind that the first and most urgent need is to reconcile the hearts of men, to bring them to fraternal agreement and cooperation, so that they may set to work upon plans and projects in keeping with the demands of Christian teaching and the needs of the present situation.

¶537 • **U.S. Bishops** • **Pastoral Letter, 1958** • The heart of the race question is moral and religious. It concerns the rights of man and our attitude toward our fellow man. If our attitude is governed by the great Christian law of love of neighbor and respect for his rights, then we can work out harmoniously the techniques for making legal, economic, and social adjustments.

¶538 • **Buddy, Charles Francis, Bishop †1966** • **Going Therefore, Teach, p. 29** • The Holy Spirit vitalizes the Church, renewing, inspiring, and directing her. The Holy Spirit perfects the body of Christ in the life of the Church, enabling her to meet the needs of each age. The mission of the third Person of the Blessed Trinity crystallizes the truths taught by Christ. The Holy Spirit forms Christ in the individual to think with the Church, to work zealously for her expansion, to be a torchlight of truth and a messenger of love.

¶539 • _____ • **Thoughts of His Heart** • Zeal for souls is love in action. The poor people, confused and starving for the milk of human kindness, cannot flee from themselves. Only in the truths of Jesus Christ, patiently taught, will they find peace or hope or stability of heart.

[9]

Reform and Renewal: the Age of Vatican II

The world of the late 1950s and early '60s was a turbulent time. Castro's Cuba was starting to become one of the world's leading troublemakers, and troops were constantly on the move in and around Israel, that beleaguered bastion of democracy in the Near East.

Hawaii had just been admitted into the Union as the fiftieth state, and John F. Kennedy became the first Roman Catholic President.

In Rome, Pope John XXIII had taken over the reins of government from the able, energetic, and long-lived Pope Pius XII. When his picture first appeared on TV, we looked at that portly, round (read "fat"), and aged man and decided that the cardinals had given us a mere transitional pope.

How wrong we were! He was a man with a sense of history, as we should have known from the name he chose. From the very start he showed himself to be a charismatic leader.

He started off with two exceptional encyclicals, *Mater et Magistra* and *Pacem in Terris*, and ended up by presiding over an ecumenical council. The Holy Spirit was very active in the Church at that time.

The Council did not spring full-grown from the mind of Pope John XXIII, but preparations had been going on for quite some time during the pontificate of Pope Pius XII. And Pope Paul VI would be the man to proclaim its decrees and start the fulfillment of them.

The Vatican Council itself was an active gathering, with the press making great issues over "liberals" and "conservatives." Both terms were relative, considering the vocation of each bishop present to conserve, or preserve, the truth of Christ. They were all dedicated to Tradition, with a capital "T," and the transmission of this to a new generation with new needs.

It is true that the "conservatives" tried to manipulate the proceedings along liturgical and Marian lines, but Pope John personally intervened to end the liturgical logjam by simply inserting the name of St. Joseph in the Canon of the Mass, thus signaling that he wanted an end to the wrangling.

The "liberals" did not get all they wanted either, but a progressive, moderate series of documents, sixteen in all, finally came from the Council.

There were four constitutions, two of them dogmatic and one, of great pastoral importance, on "The Church in the Modern World," *Gaudium et Spes*. Three declarations showed the mind of the Council Fathers in the fields of Christian education, relations with non-Christians, and a topic that interested Americans very much — religious freedom.

Nine decrees were issued to give direction to the post-Vatican II Church, and they ranged over a wide spectrum of topics from the office of bishops to ecumenism.

As with every ecumenical council in the nearly two-thousand-year history of the Catholic Church, it takes a full generation for the decisions to be tried, tested, and implemented. I think history will heap praises on Pope Paul VI for the cautious but firm direction he gave to the Church in this matter.

The fact that he angered the conservatives by going too fast, and the liberals by going too slow, proves that he took an enlightened middle way. However, we are too close to the events to begin to evaluate them properly.

The Sixteen Documents of Vatican II are available from St. Paul Editions, Boston MA 02130, and although it is now out of print, there is a valuable summary by Virginia

Heffernan, published by America Press, entitled *Outlines of the 16 Documents of Vatican II*.

We conclude this book, then, with a selection of items that lead up to or give the flavor of this exciting period, and a few general excerpts from writers* who, I think, expressed much of what was good in this century, so far, and give hope for the coming one. (*Note: There is no attempt at chronological order in this section since for some there are no birth dates, death dates, or dates of writing.)

¶540 • **Benoit, Pierre M. (1906-)** • **Jesus and the Gospel, Vol. 2, Ch. 5** • The Greek word *kerygma* is used in the New Testament to denote the first triumphant preaching that the witnesses of Christ addressed to the world to bring to its notice the "Good News" (the meaning of the word *evangelion*, gospel) of the salvation which God had just achieved in His Son and through His Spirit.

It differed from *Catechesis, Didache*, and *Didaskalia*, which followed up and taught the converted the doctrine they were to hold, in a more systematic fashion, and from *Paranesis*, which inculcated the moral obligations of their new way of life.

¶541 • **Bouyer, Louis (1913-)** • **Liturgical Piety, Ch. 6** • Sacrifice, then, is to be understood as the actual sacrifice which the Church has always intended to offer when it is assembled to celebrate the Eucharist. . . . It is a striking fact that in the most primitive and basic usages of all the ancient liturgies, the terminology of sacrifice is directly applied to what the Church does when she meets for the Eucharist.

¶542 • **Brown, Raymond E., S.S. (1928-)** • **Hermeneutics: Authoritative Interpretation by the Church** • Since the Church is the custodian of revelation and since the Scripture is the mirror of revelation, the Church has the power to determine infallibly the meaning of Scripture in matters of faith and morals.

The Church claims no absolute or direct authority over matters of biblical authorship, geography, chronology, and other scientific aspects; and so the Church has not made any dogmatic pronouncements about authorship, dating of books, unity of composition, etc.

¶543 • **Callahan, Daniel (1930-)** • **The New Church, Ch. 14** • If the concept of a "living magisterium" has any meaning at all, then it must at least mean this: one way to remain faithful to the past is to affirm the present. That is the demand which our life here today has directed to the Church's exercise of its authority. That is the cutting edge of renewal.

¶544 • **Congar, Yves, O.P. (1904-)** • **Lay People in the Church, 1:1** • Our word "lay" (*laos*) is connected with a word that for the Jews, and then for the Christians, properly meant the sacred people in opposition to the peoples who were not consecrated, a nuance of meaning that was familiar at any rate to those who spoke Greek, for the first four centuries or more.

These were the "people of God" as opposed to the heathen or the gentiles, the *goyim*.

¶545 • **Dulles, Avery, S.J. (1918-)** • **Models of the Church, Ch. 1** • The term mystery, applied to the Church, signifies many things. It implies that the Church is not fully intelligible to the finite mind of man, and that the reason for this lack of intelligibility is not the poverty but the richness of the Church itself.

Like other supernatural mysteries, the Church is known by a kind of connaturality. We cannot fully objectify the Church because we are involved in it; we know it through a kind of intersubjectivity. Furthermore, the Church pertains

to the mystery of Christ; Christ is carrying out in the Church
His plan of redemption. He is dynamically at work in the
Church through His Spirit.

¶546 • **Durrwell, Francis X. (1912-)** • **The Resurrection, 4:1** • For
Christians Christ was this divine King-Messiah. The earliest
Palestinian communities called Him "Maran" (Our Lord) and
the Greek communities proclaimed Him "Kyrios."

In the first public profession of faith in Christ we read,
"Let all the House of Israel know most certainly that God has
made both Lord and Christ this same Jesus whom you have
crucified" (Acts 2:36). In St. Peter's mind the two terms are
even more closely joined: God has made Jesus the Lord-
Messiah.

¶547 • **Ellis, John Tracy (1905-)** • **American Catholicism, Ch. 1** •
But apart from political matters, there were other similarities
between Spain and France in the New World. The same
concept, of Indian as a man whose soul had equal value in the
sight of God with that of the white man, motivated the
French Jesuits or Recollects around the Great Lakes and
through the Mississippi Valley, as much as it did their
Spanish brethren to the South.

¶548 • **Greeley, Andrew (1928-)** • **Films as Sacrament** •
Catholicism has always believed in the sacramentality of
creation. It has always held fiercely that God discloses
himself/herself to us through the experience, objects, and
people encountered in our lives — grace is everywhere, as
Karl Rahner observed. The world is deprived, not depraved,
but even in its deprived and imperfect state it still discloses
God.

The artist in the Catholic tradition is therefore one who
sees the splendor of the form in the proportion part of the
matter more clearly, more acutely, more perceptively,
perhaps more obsessively than others.

¶549 • **Grillmeier, Aloys (1910-)** • **Christ in the Christian Tradition, 1:2c** • The climax in the New Testament development of Christological thought is reached in John. His prologue to the Fourth Gospel is the most penetrating description of the career of Jesus Christ that has ever been written.

It is not without reason that the Christological formula of John 1:14 ["And the Word was made flesh and dwelt among us"] could increasingly become the most influential text in the history of dogma.

The Johannine Christology has dynamism all of its own. Christ appears as the definitive Word of God to man, as the unique and absolute *revealer*, transcending all prophets.

¶550 • **Häring, Bernard, C.SS.R. (1912-)** • **The Law of Christ, Bk 1, Ch. 1** • The principle, the norm, the center, and the goal of Christian moral theology is Christ. The law of the Christian is Christ himself in person. He alone is our Lord, our Savior. In Him we have life and therefore also the law of our life. . . .

The Christian life is following Christ, but not through mere external copying, even though it be in love and obedience. Our life must above all be a life of Christ.

¶551 • _____ • **A Sacramental Spirituality, 3:2** • Each of the seven sacraments is an expression of the original and fundamental sacrament, the love of Christ for His Church. The Church herself, in the fullest sense, is the sacrament of love. It is her task to bring the experience of the love of Christ to all men and make it visible to them, just as the well-beloved Son made the love of the heavenly Father visible in human form.

The Church is the realm in which love for one's neighbor, which comes from God and leads to God, has taken on a concrete form and must continually go on doing so.

¶552 • **Hovda, Robert (1920-)** • **Dry Bones, Ch. 1** • When we speak of liturgy, we are speaking of the act that constitutes the Church, that makes it, that identifies it as Church. We are speaking of the act in which the Church regularly finds itself, finds its meaning and its freedom and its mission.

We are speaking of the unique act in which people realize and affirm the Christ-dimension of life, the Christ-orientation and integration of life, of things and deeds. We are speaking of the deed so utterly central to the Christian life that all depends on it — and without it there is no covenant people and no Church.

¶553 • **John Paul II, Pope (1920-)** • **Redemptor Hominis, No. 24** • Man cannot live without love. He remains a being that is incomprehensible to himself; his life is senseless if love is not revealed to him, if he does not encounter love, if he does not participate intimately in it. This is why Christ the Redeemer fully reveals man to himself. If we may use the expression, this is the human dimension of the Redemption.

¶554 • **McKenzie, John L., S.J. (1910-)** • **The Power and the Wisdom, Ch. 11** • When one reviews the central theme of New Testament morality, one is depressed by a feeling of despair — despair of one's fellowman and of oneself. Is it possible? Is it practical?

One knows that one is asking God why He does not change the world into a community of love where it would not be so awfully hard to love one's neighbor as oneself.

Then one further realizes that the operation of this change is the mission God has committed to the Christian in that part of the world which is under the control of the individual person.

¶555 • _____ • **The Two-Edged Sword, Ch. 17** • Familiarity with the Old Testament has always been a key to the understanding of the New Testament. The full impact of the words of Jesus is not grasped unless we hear His words against the background of the history and the prophecy, the wisdom and the poetry of His own people.

Even in apostolic times, this was so obvious to the Apostles that they took the Old Testament with them to give to the Gentiles who knew nothing of the Jewish world. The New Testament had not been written, but the Old Testament was "background reading" for the Gentiles so that they could put the strange Gospel into its proper perspective.

¶556 • **Nedoncelle, Maurice (1905-) • Love and the Person, 1:3 •** Love dares to aspire to the conquest and explanation of all realities: the task it assumes is to take the universe as it is and transform it according to its own law. It is the ideal that, under penalty of destroying itself, recoils before nothing.

¶557 • **Oraison, Marc (1914-) • Morality for Our Time, Ch. 1 •** Now as in other great periods of the Church's history, theologians who want to translate the word, rather than study it in libraries, have a grave obligation to remain faithful — or better, to deepen their fidelity — to the word of life.

¶558 • **Rahner, Karl, S.J. (1904-1984) • Mission and Grace: Christians in the Modern World •** The apparent atrophy of the religious sense today is a passing phenomenon; in the period of vast upheaval in which we live, it was absolutely unavoidable and to be expected. . . .

Man's religious sense is ineradicable, nor can it, in the long run, be appeased by pseudo-objects provided by secular utopianism, economic, social, or cultural.

[The Church will grow] when it becomes clear everywhere that the Church desires only faith in God and love for Him, and these only as the unforced decision of the human heart, not to be induced by others.

¶559 • _____ • **The Priesthood, 9:3** • We are asking, what is the inner reality of the Catholic priesthood? It is, briefly, the continuation of the priesthood of Christ.

¶560 • _____ • **Theological Reflections, 8:4** • The *idea* of the God-man and the *acknowledgement* of Jesus and of no one else as the one, unique, and real God-man are two quite different perceptions.

Only this second perception, which is one of faith, makes one a Christian. In other words, one is a Christian only when one has grasped the uniquely concrete fact of this particular man, and once it has been grasped as God's absolute expression of himself and as God's pledge of himself to you and me.

¶561 • **Schnackenburg, Rudolf (1914-)** • **Christian Existence in the New Testament, Ch. 6** • We must not overlook an aspect which is inherent in Jesus' whole message of salvation, and also underlies the demands of the Sermon on the Mount. It is: the new eschatalogical and primally pure morality of Jesus' disciples, the undivided surrender to God, and the unlimited love of brother became possible only by God's anticipatory love and by His present work of salvation.

Perfection is not only a requirement, it is a gift as well: it is man's answer to God's work which makes man capable of perfection.

¶562 • **Schillebeeckx, Edward, O.P. (1914-)** • **Christ, the Sacrament of Encounter with God, 2:1** • Even in His humanity, Christ is the Son of God. The second person of the most holy Trinity is personally man: and this man is personally God. Therefore Christ is God in a human way, and man in a divine way.

As a man, He acts out His divine life in and according to His human existence. Everything He does as man is an act of the Son of God, a divine act in human form; an interpretation and transportation of a divine activity into a human activity.

His human love is the human embodiment of the redeeming love of God.

¶563 • Spicq, Ceslaus (1901-) • Agapē in the New Testament, Bk. 3, Ch. 5, No. 4 • Biblical theology cannot make it any more explicit, but the declaration "God is Love" says what is most proper to God and what He desires us to know about Him. He has shown us that He is love, and He wants to be recognized as He is. If we may dare to say so, charity is the property of His nature which means the most to Him.

¶564 • Suenens, Léon-Joseph Cardinal (1904-) • Co-responsibility in the Church, Ch. 2 • It is undeniable that the definition of infallibility has been so stressed in Catholic ecclesiology since 1870 that the infallibility of the Church itself, so obvious to all that no one thought it necessary to define it, was overshadowed and even neglected.

But the inerrancy of the Pope speaking *ex cathedra* was defined in reference to the infallibility of the Church. The exercise of this "prerogative" is conditioned by the various limits established by the definition itself.

¶565 • John XXIII, Pope (1881 - 1963) • Mater et Magistra, No. 1 (1961) • Mother and Teacher of all nations — such is the Catholic Church in the mind of her founder, Jesus Christ; to hold the world in an embrace of love, that even men in every age should find in her their own completeness in a higher order of living and their ultimate salvation.

She is the pillar and the ground of truth. To her her holy Founder entrusted the twofold task of giving life to her children and of teaching and guiding them, both as individuals and as nations, with maternal care. Great is their dignity, a dignity she has always guarded most zealously and held in the highest esteem.

¶566 • _____ • **Pacem in Terris, No. 112** • Justice, right reason, and the recognition of man's dignity cry out insistently for a cessation of the arms race. The stockpiles of armaments which have been built up in various countries must be reduced all around and simultaneously by all parties concerned. Nuclear weapons must be banned.

¶567 • **Ward, Maisie (1889 - 1975)** • **Caryll Houselander, p. 5 (1962)** • Christ has chosen to dwell in men, and the difficulty of discovering Him in ourselves and in others is the main testing of the Christian life. . . .

Pretending that men are not men, women are not women, but some sort of sublimated angelic beings, adds to the difficulty instead of diminishing it, for it is a manifest contradiction of the reality which surrounds us, of which we are a part.

¶568 • **Kennedy, John F. (1917 - 1963)** • **Speech, June 10, 1963** • I speak of peace at the necessary, rational end of rational men. I realize that the pursuit of peace is not as dramatic as the pursuit of war, and frequently the words of the pursuer fall on deaf ears. But we have no more urgent task.

¶569 • _____ • **Last Speech, Nov. 22, 1963 (Dallas)** • We ask, therefore, that we may be worthy of our power and responsibility, that we may exercise our strength with wisdom and restraint, and that we may achieve in our time, and for all time, the ancient vision of "peace on earth, good will toward man." That must always be our goal — and the righteousness of our cause must always underlie our strength. For as was written long ago, "Except the Lord keep the city, the watchman waketh but in vain."

¶570 • **Vann, Gerald, O.P. (1906 - 1963)** • **The Heart of Man: Vision of the Way** • The way back to God is the way of worship. If all that we are and become and do in our many-leveled life could

be made one in worship, we should be saints. Some think that
Christian morality is no more than a series of Don'ts; others a
little less ill-informed think of it as no more than a series of
Do's. These things are included, for being and doing are
interdependent; but it is being that comes first in importance;
and Christian morality tells us first of all not what we should
do, still less what we should not do, but what we should be.

¶571 • **LaFarge, John, S.J. (1880 - 1963)** • **Interracial Justice, Ch. 7** •
Christian social philosophy regards as sinful, not only actual
violations of right, but those states of mind which by
inflaming human passion and clouding human intellect
encourage such violations. For this reason, Christian social
philosophy looks upon racial prejudices, deliberately
fostered, as a sin.

Human rights, speaking in general, find their guarantee
in three major types of institutions: goverment and laws,
organic social structure, and religion.

¶572 • **Paul VI, Pope (1897 - 1978)** • **Apostolic Constitution Laudis
Canticum** • From ancient times the Church has had the custom
of celebrating each day the liturgy of the hours. In this way
the Church fulfills the Lord's command to pray without
ceasing, both offering its praise to God the Father and
interceding for the salvation of the world.

The hymn of praise that is sung through all the ages in the
heavenly places and was brought by the high priest, Jesus
Christ, into this land of exile has been continued by the
Church with constant fidelity over many centuries, in a
variety of forms.

The liturgy of the hours has developed into the prayer of
the local Church, a prayer offered at regular intervals and in
appointed places. It was seen as a kind of necessary
complement to the fullness of divine worship that is
contained in the eucharistic sacrifice, by means of which that

worship might overflow into the daily life of the Church. It is the prayer of the whole People of God.

¶573 • _____ • **Mysterium Fidei, No. 1** • The Mystery of Faith, that is, the ineffable gift of the Eucharist that the Catholic Church received from Christ, her Spouse, as a pledge of His immense love, is something that she has always devoutly guarded as her most precious treasure, and during the Second Vatican Council she professed her faith and veneration in a new and solemn declaration.

¶574 • _____ • **Sermon at Nazareth, 1964** • Nazareth is a kind of school where we may begin to discover what Christ's life was really like, and even to understand His Gospel. Here we can observe and ponder the simple appeal of the way God's Son came to be known, profound yet full of hidden meaning. Here we can sense and take account of the conditions and circumstances that surrounded and affected His life on earth — the places, the tenor of the times, the culture, the language, religious customs, and, in brief, everything which Jesus used to make himself known to the world.

¶575 • **Vatican Council II (1962 - 1965)** • **Dei Verbum, Nos.3, 4 (1965)** • God sent His Son, the eternal Word, who enlightens all men, to dwell among men and make known to them the innermost things of God. . . .
The Christian dispensation, because it is the new and definitive covenant, will never pass away, and no new public revelation is any longer to be looked for before the manifestation in glory of our Lord Jesus Christ.

¶576 • _____ • **Gaudium et Spes, No. 10** • The Church believes that Christ died and rose for all, and can give man light and strength through His Spirit to fulfill his highest calling; His is the only name under heaven by which man can be saved.

The Church believes that the center and the goal of all human history is found in her Lord and Master. Underlying all changes there are many things that do not change; they have their ultimate foundation in Christ, who is "the same yesterday, today and for ever."

¶577 • _____ • **Gaudium et Spes, No. 20** • God has called man, and still calls him, to be united in his whole being in perpetual communion with himself in the immortality of the Divine Life. This victory has been gained for us by the Risen Christ, who by His own death freed man from death. . . .

By entering into the Paschal mystery and being made like Christ in death, he will also look forward, strong in hope, to the Resurrection.

¶578 • _____ • **Gaudium et Spes, No. 37** • Man, redeemed by Christ and made a new creation in the Holy Spirit, can and must love the very things created by God. For he receives them from God and sees and reveres them as coming from the hand of God. . . .

The Word of God, through whom all things were made, himself became man and lived in the world of man. As perfect man He entered into the history of the world, taking it upon himself and bringing it into unity as its Head. He reveals to us that God is love, and at the same time teaches us that the fundamental law of human perfection, and therefore of the transformation of the world, is the new commandment of love.

¶579 • _____ • **Gaudium et Spes, No. 78** • Peace is not merely the absence of war or the simple maintenance of a balance of power between forces, nor can it be imposed at the dictates of absolute power.

Peace is called, rightly and properly, a work of justice. It is the product of order, the order implanted in human society by its divine founder. It is to be realized in practice as men hunger and thirst for ever more complete and perfect justice.

¶580 • _____ **• Lumen Gentium, No. 9 •** The Israel of old was already called the Church of God while it was on pilgrimage through the desert. So, the New Israel, as it makes its way in this present age, seeking a city that is to come, a city that will remain, is also known as the Church of Christ, for He acquired it by His own Blood, filled it with His Spirit, and equipped it with appropriate means to be a visible and social unity.

God has called together the assembly of those who in faith look on Jesus, the author of salvation and the principle of unity and peace, and so has established the Church to be for each and all the visible sacrament of this unity which brings salvation.

¶581 • _____ **• Lumen Gentium, No. 12 •** The whole company of the faithful, who have an anointing by the Spirit, cannot err in faith. They manifest this distinctive characteristic of theirs in the supernatural instinct of faith (*sensus fidei*) of the whole people when, from the bishops to the most ordinary lay person among the faithful, they display a universal agreement on matters of faith and morals.

¶582 • _____ **• Lumen Gentium, No. 16 •** Eternal salvation is open to those who, through no fault of their own, do not know Christ and His Church but seek God with a sincere heart, and under the inspiration of grace try in their lives to do His will, made known to them by the dictate of their conscience. Nor does Divine Providence deny the aids necessary for salvation to those who, without blame on their part, have not yet reached an explicit belief in God, but strive to lead a good life, under the influence of God's grace.

¶583 • _____ • **Lumen Gentium, No. 48** • Lifted above the earth, Christ drew all things to himself. Rising from the dead, He sent His life-giving Spirit upon His disciples, and through the Holy Spirit He established His Body, which is the Church, as the universal sacrament of salvation.

Seated at the right hand of His Father, He works unceasingly in the world to draw men into the Church and through it to join them more closely to himself, nourishing them with His own Body and Blood, and so making them share in His own life of glory.

¶584 • _____ • **Sacrosanctum Concilium, No. 5** • The work of man's redemption of God's perfect glory was foreshadowed by God's mighty deeds among the people of the Old Covenant. It was brought to fulfillment by Christ the Lord, especially through the paschal mystery of His blessed passion, resurrection from the dead and ascension into glory.

By dying He destroyed our death, by rising He restored our life. . . .

¶585 • **Levie, Jean (1885 - 1966)** • **The Bible, Word of God, Ch. 9** • We cannot justify from a theological standpoint the genuine, authentic development of dogma by comparison with the sometimes still rudimentary and, in a sense, still incomplete character of some of our scriptural texts, unless that we admit that these texts, lived in the Christian life of the Church, and clarified by the whole of Catholic dogma as it has developed, have revealed to the Church, guided by the Spirit, a richer, deeper, more complete meaning than that which can be logically deduced from the actual words by a strict, critical exegesis. It is this more complete meaning which has been rightly called the plenary sense of Scripture.

¶586 • **Adam, Karl (1876 - 1966)** • **The Christ of Faith, Ch. 14** • As man, Christ is one with mankind; indeed with the entire created world, at whose head He stands. As God, He stands in a union of substance with His Father, from whom He comes, and with the Holy Spirit, in which He encounters the Father.

Standing in the world, one with the world, He towers up into the heart of the Godhead, He is God himself, one with the Father and the Holy Spirit.

¶587 • _____ **• The Spirit of Catholicism, Ch. 3 •** When we define the Church as essentially the Kingdom of God and the Body of Christ, it follows as her first particular attribute that she is supernatural and heavenly. The Church is ordinated toward the invisible, spiritual, and heavenly. But the Church is not only visible. Because she is the Kingdom of God, she is no haphazard collection of individuals, but an ordered system of regularly subordinated parts. . . .

In her, the divine is objectivized, is incarnated in the community, and precisely and only in so far as it is a community.

¶588 • _____ **• The Spirit of Catholicism, Ch. 3 •** The Incarnation is for Christians the foundation and the planting of that new communion which we call the Church. The Body of Christ and the Kingdom of God came into being as objective reality at the moment when the Word was made Flesh.

¶589 • Murray, John Courtney, S.J. (1904 - 1967) • We Hold These Truths, Pt. 1, Ch. 1 • The philosophy of the Bill of Rights was also tributary to the tradition of natural law, to the idea that man has certain original responsibilities precisely as man, antecedent to his status as citizen. These responsibilities are creative of rights which inhere in man antecedent to any act of government; therefore they are not granted by government and they cannot be surrendered to government.

They are as inalienable as they are inherent. Their proximate source is in nature, and in history, insofar as history bears witness to the nature of man. Their ultimate source, as the Declaration of Independence states, is in God, the Creator of nature and the Master of history.

¶590 • Guardini, Romano (1885 - 1968) • The Church and the Catholic, Ch. 4 • In the Church, eternity enters time.

Even in the Church, it is true, there is much which is temporal. No one acquainted with her history will deny it. But the substance of her doctrine, the fundamental facts which determine the structure of her religious system, and the general outlines of her moral code and her ideal of perfection, transce id time.

¶591 • _____ • The Lord, 2:3 • We must try to understand something of the uniqueness of the Sermon on the Mount: its revolutionary tidings; the energy with which it insists upon the progression from the outer, specific act of virtue to the inner, all-permeating state of virtue; its demand for identification-of-self-with-neighbor as the sole measure for purity of intent, and consequently, its definition of love as the essence of man's new disposition.

¶592 • _____ • The Spirit of the Liturgy, Ch. 7 • The Church forgives everything more readily than an attack on truth. She knows that if a man fails, but leaves truth unimpaired, he will find his way back again. But if he attacks the vital principle, then the sacred order of life is demolished.

Moreover, the Church has constantly viewed with the deepest distrust every ethical conception of truth and dogma. Any attempt to base the truth of a dogma on its practical value is essentially un-Catholic. The Church represents truth — dogma — as an absolute fact, based upon itself, independent of all confirmation from the moral or even the practical sphere.

Truth is truth because it is truth.

¶593 • Cerfaux, Lucien (1883 - 1968) • Christian Theology of St. Paul, Ch. 6 • It is rare for Paul to say "Jesus" and nothing more. However, he sometimes does it, usually in a passage which recalls the earliest form of faith, either the parousia or the death and resurrection. . . . Here the apostle is harking back implicitly to the manner of speaking of the Palestine community, of those who were witnesses of the life of Jesus.

In all there are ten such passages in the epistles. We may bring them together by saying that all the texts lead us back to the primitive formulas: the name of "Jesus" represents the historical fact and is a reminder of the very beginnings of the rise of Christianity.

¶594 • Merton, Thomas (Father Louis, O.C.S.O., 1915 - 1968) • Conjectures of a Guilty Bystander, Pt. 2 • Since I am a Catholic, I believe, of course, that my Church guarantees for me the highest spiritual freedom. I would not be a Catholic if I did not believe this. I would not be a Catholic if the Church were merely an organization, a collective institution with rules and laws demanding external conformity from its members.

I see the laws of the Church, and all the various ways in which she exercises her teaching authority and her jurisdiction, as subordinate to the Holy Spirit and the law of love. . . . It is in Christ and in His Spirit that true freedom is found, and the Church is His Body, living by His Spirit.

¶595 • _____ • Disputed Questions — The Power of Love • Love is the key to the meaning of life. It is at the same time transformation in Christ and the discovery of Christ. As we grow in love and in unity with those who are loved by Christ, that is to say, everyone, we become more and more capable of apprehending and obscurely grasping something of the tremendous reality of Christ in the world, Christ in ourselves, and Christ in our fellow man.

¶596 • **Dondeyne, Albert (1901-)** • **Faith and the World, Ch. 9, No. 4**
• Christianity is not an economic theory but a religion and an
ethics of religious inspiration. It is not impossible that in
particular circumstances, a far-reaching planning and
"collectivization" of economic life might not be almost the
only way to make undeveloped countries attain a relatively
high degree of prosperity in a fairly short time.

In any case, the question is not a religious but an
economic problem and is to be solved by the economist and
not the theologian. The only thing faith demands is that
whatever economic policy a country may choose, it must
respect man and recognize the inalienable rights and values
of the human person.

¶597 • **Alberione, James (1884   )** • **Mary, Hope of the World (concl.)**
• Through the Gospel, devotion to Mary became widespread
among Christians, and we have the first manifestations of
Marian devotions.

After the Council of Ephesus, love and veneration for the
Mother of God grew considerably by reason of the abundance
of literature defending, explaining, illustrating the dogma of
Mary's motherhood.

¶598 • **Sheed, Frank (1897 - 1981)** • **What Difference Does Jesus
Make?, p. 192** • Of what happened on that first day [Easter] and
on the forty days (Acts 1:3) in which He came and went
among them before His Ascension, the Evangelists selected,
from their own memories and the accounts of others,
incidents which they saw as specially significant, with no
attempt to harmonize them. But all four give the same
outline. There was the tomb found empty on the Sunday
morning; there were appearances to various women,
disciples, apostles.

¶599 • **Maritain, Jacques (1882 - 1973)** • **Man and the State, 4:4, 5** •
For a philosophy which recognizes Fact alone (positivism)
the notion of Value — I mean Value objectively true in itself
— is not conceivable. How, then, can one claim rights if one
does not believe in values? If the affirmation of the intrinsic
value and dignity of man is nonsense, the affirmation of the
natural rights of man is nonsense also. . . .

Natural law deals with the rights and duties which are
connected in a *necessary* manner with the first principle, "Do
good and avoid evil." This is why the precepts of the
unwritten law are in themselves or in the nature of things
(not necessarily man's knowledge of them) universal and
invariable.

¶600 • _____ • **Moral Philosophy, 2:15** • That it is possible
for man to attain absolute happiness is not a datum of
philosophy or of reason, but of Christian faith. Reason by
itself, if we consider not the infinite power of God, of course,
but the human condition, would have ample grounds to make
us doubt the possibility.

¶601 • **Journet, Charles (1891 - 1975)** • **The Church of the Word
Incarnate, Ch. 1, No. 3** • First the Word is sent from heaven into
our flesh, and then, having promised the help of the Spirit,
He sends His own disciples into the world: "As the Father
has sent Me, I also send you" (Jn. 20:21). Hence the perfect
regime of the Church militant involves a doubly visible
mediation: that of the Incarnation and that of the hierarchy.

¶602 • **Von Hildebrand, Dietrich (1889 - 1977)** • **Transformation in
Christ, Ch. 3** • The readiness to change is an essential aspect of
the Christian's basic relation with God; it forms the core of
our response to the merciful love of God which bends down
upon us: "With eternal charity has God loved us; so He has
drawn us lifted from the earth, to His merciful Heart"
(Antiphon: Feast of the Sacred Heart).

To us all has the inexorable yet beatifying call of Christ been addressed, "Come, follow Me." Nor do we follow it unless, relinquishing everything, we say with St. Paul, "Lord, what would You have me do?" (Acts 9:6).

¶603 • **Sheen, Fulton, Archbishop (1895 - 1979)** • **Wisdom for Welfare, Preface** • In the streets of the Roman world, of which Israel was but a conquered part, there stands an exultant woman proclaiming to all the world the tidings of her emancipation. "He that is mighty has done great things for me" (Lk. 1:46). It was a representative voice, not only of Israel, but of womanhood and the world. It was the clarion call of a long-repressed sex claiming its right and hailing its emancipation. . . .

Not in her times alone, but in her for all times, woman would find her glory and her honor. They could not call her Jew nor Greek nor Roman; not successful nor beautiful, but "blessed," that is, holy. And blessed she is because by giving birth to the God-Man she broke down the trammels of nationality and race. Her Son was cosmopolitan. He is MAN *par excellence*. And she is The WOMAN because she is the Mother of God.

¶604 • **Wyszynski, Stefan, Cardinal †1981** • Man is too noble to serve anyone but God.

¶605 • **Cooke, Terence Cardinal (1921 - 1983)** • **Respect Life Month Letter, Oct. 1983*** • At this grace-filled time of my life, as I experience suffering in union with Jesus Our Lord and Redeemer, I offer gratitude to Almighty God for giving me the opportunity to continue my apostolate on behalf of life. I thank each one of you . . . for what you have done and will do on behalf of human life. May we never yield to indifference or claim helplessness when innocent human life is threatened or when human rights are denied. [*Cardinal Cooke died on Oct. 6, 1983.]

¶606 • Day, Dorothy (1898 - 1984) • The Long Loneliness, Pt. 3 •
"All men are brothers." How often we hear this refrain, the
rallying call that strikes a response in every human heart.
These are the words of Christ, "Call no man master for you
are all brothers." It is a revolutionary call which has even
been put to music.

The last movement of Beethoven's Ninth Symphony has
that great refrain, "All men are brothers." Going to the
people is the purest and best act in Christian tradition and
revolutionary tradition and is the beginning of world
brotherhood.

¶607 • _____ • On Pilgrimage, Mar. 8, 1948 • I try to practice
the presence of God after the manner of Blessed Lawrence,
and pray without ceasing, as St. Paul advised. He might even
have had women in mind. But he himself was active enough,
weaving goat's hair into tents and sailcloth to earn a living,
and preaching nights and Sundays.

So I am trying to learn to recall my soul like the straying
creature it is as it wanders off over and over again during the
day, and lift my heart to the Blessed Mother and the saints,
since my occupations are the lowly and humble ones, as were
theirs.

¶608 • Doherty, Catherine de Hueck (1900 - 1985) • Poustinia, 1:1 •
It seems strange to say, but what can help modern man find
the answers to his own mystery and the mystery of Him in
whose image he is created is silence, solitude — in a word,
the desert.

True silence is the search of a man for God; / True silence
is the speech of lovers; / True silence is the key to the
immense, flaming Heart of God; / True silence is a
suspension bridge that a soul in love with God builds to cross
the dark, frightening gullies of its own mind, that impede its
way to God.

Index of Authors

The first number, in parentheses, refers to the century in which the author flourished; the second, and those following, to the paragraphs as numbered in the text, not the page. (Note: These are alphabetized according to common Catholic usage, not according to library rules.)

A

Abélard, Peter (12th), 227
Acton, Lord, (19th), 462
Adam, Karl, (20th), 586-588
Adam of St.-Victor (12th), 230
Aelred, St. (12th), 228, 229
Alain de Lille (12th), 253
Alberione, James (20th), 597
Albert the Great, St. (13th), 285
Alcuin of York (8th), 200
Alexander I, Pope St. (2nd), 16
Alfred the Great, King (9th), 209
Allen, William, Cardinal (16th), 361
Alphonsus Liguori, St. (17th), 414
Alphonsus Rodriguez, St. (17th), 366
Ambrose, St. (4th), 99-107
Andrew of Crete, St. (8th), 194
Angela Merici, St. (16th), 328
Anon.: *Anima Christi* (14th), 294
Anselm, St. (11th), 218, 219
Anthony Mary Claret, St. (19th), 435
Anthony of Padua, St. (13th), 261
Antonio, Silvio (16th), 364
Aphraates (4th), 70
Aristedes (2nd), 19
Arnobius the Elder (4th), 71
Asterius of Amasea, St. (4th), 114
Athanasius, St. (4th), 78-81

Athenagoras (2nd), 27
Augustine, St. (5th), 126-138

B

Baker, Augustine (17th), 376
Barbour, John (14th), 305
Barnabas (anon.) (2nd), 18
Basil the Great, St. (4th), 83-86
Bede the Venerable, St. (8th), 195, 196
Belloc, Hilaire (20th), 522, 523
Benedict, St. (6th), 168, 169
Benedict XII, Pope (14th), 295
Benedict XIV, Pope (18th), 404
Benedict XV, Pope (20th), 477
Benedict Joseph Labre, St (18th), 415
Benoit, Pierre (20th), 450
Benson, Robert Hugh (20th), 475, 476
Berengarius of Tours (11th), 217
Bernard of Clairvaux, St. (12th), 238-246
Bernard of Cluny, St. (12th), 237
Bernard of Morlas (12th), 231
Bernardine of Siena, St. (15th), 311, 312
Bérulle, Pierre de (17th), 374
Blois, Louis de, Bl. (16th), 343
Boethius (6th), 165, 166

General Index

(Numbers refer to numbered paragraphs, not pages.)

M